Policy Innovation
in State Government

Policy Innovation in State Government

DAVID C. NICE

Iowa State University Press / Ames

David C. Nice is professor and chair of the Department of Political Science, Washington State University, Pullman. He is the author of *Federalism: The Politics of Intergovernmental Relations* and numerous articles on state politics and public policy-making.

© 1994 Iowa State University Press, Ames, Iowa 50014

∞ Printed on acid-free paper in the United States of America

First edition, 1994

Library of Congress Cataloging-in-Publication Data

Nice, David C.
    Policy innovation in state government / David C. Nice. — 1st ed.
       p.   cm.
    Includes bibliographical references and index.
    ISBN 0-8138-0658-5 (acid-free paper)
    1. State governments — United States.   2. Policy sciences.
  I. Title.
  JK2431.N53   1994
  353.9 — dc20   93-24017

This book is dedicated to the late Jack Walker,

who taught us all a lot about innovation.

C O N T E N T S

P R E F A C E

For as long as governments have existed, people have wondered why those governments chose particular policies. Was a course of action adopted to divert attention from some other problem, because someone had influence at court, after a thorough study of the damage caused by some phenomenon, or because money was available to spend? Was a course of action not taken because it was too expensive, because no one thought about it, or because it ran counter to the beliefs of public officials? There has never been a shortage of impressionistic explanations for the policy decisions made by governments.

In the late 1950s and early 1960s, however, social scientists began doing relatively systematic research on a large scale in hopes of explaining why governments chose specific policies. While most of that early research dealt with patterns of government spending, some researchers began to focus on why governments decide to do something new rather than simply doing more (or less) of what they have been doing for years. This study is a continuation of that effort.

This book emerged from a series of studies of individual policy innovations and an effort to make sense of a striking finding: state characteristics that helped to account for some innovations were of no value in accounting for others. I have tried, therefore, to attack two problems. First, I have taken a series of policy innovations and sought to determine what factors help to account for those individual innovations. Second, and more important, I have tried to determine why some innovations appear to be related to some state characteristics, such as ideology, while other innovations are not. The latter effort is necessarily more in the nature of proposing hypotheses rather than offering conclusive proof in view of the limited number of innovations included in the analysis.

I hope that this book will be of value to people who are interested in public policy-making, whether researchers, students, or citizens. Consequently, I have included statistical material that may be of interest to researchers but will be relatively incomprehensible to many other people. I have tried, however, to discuss the findings in sufficient detail that people with little or no statistical background will be able to follow what was done and what was found. In a similar manner, in the discussions of individual innovations I have tried to give the reader who is not familiar with the specific issues some feel for what is at stake but have not provided a complete overview of all the related phenomena, as in the case of education reform. However, I have included references that will enable readers to obtain a more general grounding in whatever issue is of greater interest to them. Following Thoreau, I ask readers to "accept such portions as apply to them. I trust that none will stretch the seams in putting on the coat, for it may do good service to him whom it fits."[1]

A number of people deserve thanks for help they provided, deliberately or not, in the development of this book. I have borrowed ideas and insights from a wide variety of scholars, most of whom are recognized in the notes and references. Several whose contributions are not reflected there in proportion to their value include Joel Aberbach, Sam Eldersveld, Tom Hone, Kent Jennings, Tom Lauth, George Simpson, Frank Thompson, and especially Jeff Cohen, who has been an unfailing source of ideas, encouragement, and friendship over the years. Lynda Billings and Bonnie Goodrich also deserve special thanks for typing numerous revisions and catching a number of my mistakes in the process.

I also thank the Earhart Foundation for financial support that was of tremendous value in speeding the completion of this work. In a time when funding for social science research is difficult to find, the Earhart Foundation manages to continue its tradition of support for scholarship.

Finally, I want to thank a number of journals and presses for their kind permission to draw upon some of my previously published work: "Teacher Competency Testing as a Policy Innovation," *Policy Studies Journal* 13 (1984): 45–54; "State Deregulation of intimate Behavior," *Social Science Quarterly* 69 (1988): 203–211, reprinted (with revisions) by permission of the University of Texas Press; "Incremental and Nonincremental Policy Responses: The States and the Railroads," *Policy* 20 (1987): 145–156; "State Financed Property Tax Relief to Individuals: A Research Note," *Western Political Quarterly* 40 (1987): 179–185, reprinted (with revisions) by permission of the University of Utah, copyright holder; "State Support for Constitutional Balanced Budget Requirements," *Journal of Politics* 48 (1986): 134–142, reprinted (with revisions) by permission of the University of Texas Press; "Sunset Laws and Legislative Vetoes in the States," *Journal of State Government* 58 (1985): 27–32; "The States and Passenger Rail Service," *Transportation Research* 21A (1987): 385–390, reprinted (with revisions) by permission of Pergamon Press; "Political Equality and Campaign Finance in the American States," *Social Science Quarterly* 65 (1984): 1104–1111, reprinted (with revisions) by permission of the University of Texas Press.

NOTES

See Bibliography for full reference.

1. Thoreau (1976: 4).

Policy Innovation
in State Government

1

Innovation Research

Introduction

In the concluding chapter of *Walden,* Henry Thoreau reflects on his decision to leave Walden Pond:

> It is remarkable how easily and insensibly we fall into a particular route, and make a beaten track for ourselves. I had not lived there a week before my feet wore a path from my door to the pondside. . . . The surface of the earth is soft and impressible by the feet of men; and so with the paths which the mind travels.[1]

Examples of the ease with which people and their institutions develop habitual patterns of behavior are everywhere. Many people develop religious affiliations at an early age and never seriously consider joining another denomination. People become fans of a baseball team, and the loyalty often persists through losing seasons and the departure of the players on the team when the loyalty was originally formed. In a similar fashion, party loyalties often emerge at an early age and display considerable durability over time, with some exceptions. Individual tastes in music, food, recreation, and countless other things seem to fall into the beaten track described by Thoreau; what lies beyond the track often receives little or no attention.

Our institutions often display the same tendency to develop habitual behavior patterns. In some companies, workers regularly socialize together, but workers in other firms rarely associate with one another outside work. Those social patterns often persist even after significant turnover in the work force. Many churches become accustomed to a

3

particular order of service, even to the point of particular musical arrangements and lyrics for hymns. Changing to a new hymnal with a new liturgy and new or revised hymns is often resisted, sometimes bitterly.

The legacy of the past is also visible in government. Once government organizations are created, they have a remarkable ability to survive, even in the face of repeated attacks by their adversaries.[2] Patterns of public spending are relatively persistent; high-spending states or agencies in one year tend to be high spenders in other years.[3] Once policy commitments are established or administrative procedures routinized, they are often difficult to change.

Not all habits are bad, of course. Stability and predictability have many virtues. Most people lack the time, energy, and inclination to reexamine their political affiliations, religious beliefs, or artistic tastes on a regular basis. Few organizations, whether government agencies, businesses, or social clubs, are inclined to reassess their goals, procedures, and policies very often. Most of us can appreciate the value of knowing what to expect from day to day.

Although habit and continuity are major features of human existence for individuals and institutions, changes do occur. New fashions, political movements, and new technology contribute to changes in individual behavior. Businesses adopt new methods of production and employee relations. Athletic teams change strategies and abandon genuine grass in favor of synthetic turf. Governments manage to shake off their attachments to the past and try new programs or procedures. Even the American states have broken new ground on many occasions. This study explores innovation in the states.

The remainder of this chapter is devoted to several concerns. First, a definition of innovation is offered. Second, the major themes of the innovation literature are reviewed. Third, the charge that the states are backward, along with the obstacles that typically confront innovations, is explored. Finally, a preview of the remainder of the book is presented.

The Concept of Innovation

Scholars from a variety of disciplines, including political science, sociology, and economics, have been studying innovations for many years. Not surprisingly, different researchers have defined *innovation* in somewhat different ways. The variations in definitions are comparatively modest, at least relative to the varying definitions found for some concepts in the social sciences; nevertheless, the differences are sufficiently noteworthy to merit examination. The choice of definitions may reflect the needs of particular researchers; the definition used for this inquiry may not be suitable for other purposes.

The most general definition of *innovation* ("change," "reform"), the one used in this analysis, is "a program or policy which is new to the state adopting it, no matter how old the program may be or how many other states have adopted it."[4] The fundamental characteristic of an innovation is its qualitative difference from existing routines and practices. The growth of a state's budget from $950 million to $1 billion dollars may have great symbolic significance, with newspaper headlines proclaiming or denouncing the "State's First Billion Dollar Budget," but reaching that threshold would not constitute an innovation. By the same token, a marginal increase in an agency's labor force would not constitute an innovation if the new personnel are simply used to continue long-established activities and practices.

In operational terms, the distinction between an innovation and a marginal adjustment in ongoing operations is not always clear. How large must a "marginal adjustment" be to constitute an innovation? No precise guidelines exist, but March and Simon offer a helpful clue: "Innovation [is] present when change requires the devising and evaluation of new performance programs that have not previously been part of the organization's repertory and cannot be introduced by a simple application of programmed switching roles."[5] An innovation, in this perspective, is not simply adding more resources to current operations or shifting emphases among different programs that have existed for a considerable period. Innovation involves the introduction of new decision rules, new technology, new approaches to organizing, or new goals.[6]

Innovation, in the sense of adopting a new program or policy, is distinct from the invention or creation of a new program.[7] A novel approach may originate in a single state, another government (national, state, local, or foreign), or the private sector. Nevertheless, officials in a state must decide whether to adopt a new approach, regardless of whether the idea originated in the state or elsewhere.

A number of analysts have proposed and used somewhat different definitions of innovation over the years. Mohr regards it as "the *successful* introduction into an applied situation of means or ends that are new to that situation."[8] For my purposes, the inclusion of *success* or *impact* in the definition creates potentially significant problems. Success may mean different things to different people. Success may mean achievement of stated goals, such as a reduction in the crime rate. Success to public officials may mean the preservation of their political careers. Success to some people may mean the symbolic recognition of their concerns or beliefs.[9] Program benefits may emerge quickly or slowly and gradually.

For my purposes, then, the question whether an innovation is successful will be regarded as beyond the scope of this inquiry. This is not to say that the effectiveness of policy innovations is an unimportant matter; assessing the impact of policies and reforms is an important task for policy researchers.[10] The focus of this analysis, however, is on why innovations are adopted or rejected. The results of the innovations merit evaluation, but that task will be left to other studies.

Other analysts emphasize that innovations must be "perceived to be new by the relevant unit of adoption."[11] While the perceptions of decision makers are a topic worthy of study, emphasizing perceptions for this study would create several problems. First, policymakers in the same jurisdiction may not agree on the newness of a proposal. Teacher competency testing, for example, may be regarded as a drastic reform by some legislators, but others may regard it as an incremental expansion of long-established teacher certification programs and professional licensing procedures for other professions. If different decision makers in the same state have differing views regarding whether a proposal constitutes a break with the past or a marginal adjustment of established operations, is that proposal simultaneously an innovation and not an innovation?

A second complication arising from the emphasis on the perceptions of decision makers occurs when comparisons across organizations are made. If officials in state A regard a property tax relief proposal as a fundamental change in the state tax system and officials in state B consider an identical proposal a minor extension of other tax exemptions and deductions, the proposal in A would be regarded as an innovation, and the identical initiative in B would not. Given that a common political strategy involved presenting new initiatives as minor revisions or extensions of old programs,[12] variations in officials' perceptions may reflect little more than differing tactical choices in some cases.

Finally, a number of the innovations examined here were adopted by some states a decade or more ago. The perceptions of officials when these decisions were made are virtually impossible to retrieve. For my purposes, then, the perceptions of officials regarding whether a proposal is a significant break with the past are beyond the scope of this study.

One other view of innovation, which will not be utilized in this analysis, regards innovation as the first or an early adoption of a new program.[13] Since many innovations diffuse slowly,[14] a state may be slow (in an absolute sense) to adopt a new policy but still be embarking on what for that state is a significant initiative. Moreover, even a state that acts slowly in an absolute sense may still move before other states that are slower still.

Bear in mind that although public-sector innovations often include new organizations or new services, with an accompanying increase in the size and scope of government, not all innovations take that form. The repeal of state laws requiring racial segregation in public facilities involved reforms that reduced the scope of state activity; state authority was no longer used to enforce racial separation. Deregulation of airlines was a policy that reduced national governmental authority, but as a new approach and new philosophy, deregulation still constitutes an innovation. The distinctive feature of an innovation is the quality of being new to the organization adopting the program, regardless of whether the result is an increase or decrease in the scope of governmental activity.

Note too that many innovations have little or no impact on the magnitude of governmental activity. Changing from a personnel system that hires public employees because of their political connections to a system that hires people because of their job skills has relatively little direct impact on the overall extent of public-sector activity but still constitutes an innovation.[15] Direct deposit of Social Security checks did not substantially affect the size or scope of Social Security programs but was a change that increased the convenience and safety of program beneficiaries.

This study, then, will regard innovations as policies or programs new to the state adopting them, even if the policy was first adopted in other states years earlier. Changes that reduce the scope of governmental activity or leave it unchanged are just as worthy of analysis as innovations that expand governmental activity. Whether the innovations are perceived to be new by the officials adopting them and whether the innovations are successful will be beyond the scope of this analysis.

Innovation as a Focus of Research

If the innovation literature has developed a general consensus on the concept of innovation, albeit with some variations on the theme, the same cannot be said for the approaches to exploring innovation, examining a variety of aspects of innovations in a variety of contexts. Not surprisingly, the conclusions have not always been consistent.[16]

One fundamental dimension of variation among innovation studies involves the unit of analysis. A number of studies have examined adoption of innovations by individuals, as in the case of farmers deciding to use new agricultural technologies or rural peasants adopting improved hygiene practices.[17] Much of that literature is in the fields of sociology and education and involves individuals making decisions that at least in the immediate sense primarily affect themselves and their families. Of course, the cumulative effects of those individual decisions may have far-reaching consequences for a nation's health, safety, and economic development.

Other research has focused on organizations.[18] This literature has roots in the fields of organization theory, economics, public administration, business administration, and other disciplines. It has explored innovation by businesses, public agencies, and nonprofit organizations, ranging from management reforms and utilization of new technologies to changes in basic organizational goals.

A third body of innovation research has utilized governments (national, state, or local) as the unit of analysis.[19] Not surprisingly, much of this work has been done by political scientists, although scholars from other fields, particularly sociology, have made notable contributions. Some of this research has probed the interactions between different levels of government in shaping change, as in the case of one level of government adopting a change that encourages or discourages similar or related action by another level.[20]

While the preceding three groups of studies all focus on the unit that decides whether to adopt a reform, a fourth body of research analyzes change agents, those actors who seek to encourage the adoption of reform by others.[21] Change agents may be public employees who seek to change individual behavior, as in the case of public health workers who encourage people to adopt safe sex practices. Other agents include consultants and sales representatives who encourage businesses to use different management techniques or purchase new equipment. Still other agents are policy entrepreneurs; they occupy a wide variety of positions, from interest-group leadership to academic posts to offices in government, but they all work to shape the policy decisions of government.[22]

Researchers may incorporate elements of two or more units of analysis in the same study. An examination of organizational innovation may include the role of change agents with many other factors. A governmental innovation, such as extending voting rights to women, is followed by millions of decisions by women whether to be individual innovators — whether to engage in a novel activity at the time the suffrage is expanded. Different units of analysis are sometimes incorporated in the same study or at least into interrelated studies.

A second general dimension of variation in the innovation literature centers on the relative emphasis on innovativeness as a general, stable characteristic and variations in the propensity to innovate across different types of decisions or over time.[23] Some studies have emphasized general innovativeness, in the sense of being relatively quick to adopt new practices or policies of a wide variety.[24] These studies correspond to the broad notion that some governments (or organizations or people) often seem to be among the first to try something new, while others typically seem to be slow to change.

Other research, however, has argued that propensities to innovate may vary from one type of change to another. According to this perspective, governments (or organizations or people) that are quick to adopt new civil rights programs, for example, may not be similarly quick to enact educational reforms.[25] The evidence provides considerable support for that position.

The disagreement between the general-trait perspective and the issue-specific perspective, based on existing evidence, is not so much a matter of right versus wrong as differing research interests. The evidence on the American states shows that

1. When the speed with which the states have adopted a wide variety of innovations is averaged across all those innovations, some states clearly emerge as generally faster to do new things than others.[26]
2. When the speed with which states innovate in one policy arena is compared to the speed with which they innovate in another, states that are leaders in one arena do not necessarily behave in the same way regarding another type of policy.[27]

The first body of work addresses the questions Are some states (or other units) generally faster to adopt or more inclined to adopt new programs or practices than others? If so, which states? The second body addresses the questions Are some states (or other units) faster or more inclined to adopt new initiatives in the field of civil rights or law enforcement or whatever than other states? If so, which states? Similar tensions exist in other fields of research: overall intelligence versus capabilities of more specific types, such as solving mathematical problems; overall military capabilities versus the strength of strategic nuclear forces. Being able to develop broad generalizations regarding overall tendencies to innovate is a useful contribution to the literature, as is the exploration of particular innovations or clusters of innovations that may or may not conform to broader inclinations regarding innovativeness in general.

Inclinations regarding change may vary over time[28] and from one policy area to another. Being a leader at one point in history does not ensure a continuing position among the first to adopt new initiatives. In a similar fashion, units may be slow to do anything new in one era and shift to being relative innovators in another era.

Research that explores patterns of adoption across units has varied in the emphases placed on the timing of adoptions and the geographical pattern of the spread of innovations. Some researchers place considerable emphasis on time sequence. Many changes begin very slowly; only a few units adopt them over a span of several years. Gradually the pace of adoption accelerates until comparatively few nonadopting units remain, at which point the number of adoptions per year typically declines. The timing of many innovations, then, corresponds to a learning-curve distribution or some similar function,[29] although numerous exceptions exist.[30]

Other research emphasizes geographical patterns. Walker's analysis of innovation in the states found considerable evidence of geographical clustering.[31] Most of the states in a region would generally not adopt a new program until the regional leader acted. However, the regional patterns began to blur somewhat by the middle decades of the twentieth century.[32]

While most research focuses on the adoption of innovations, some analysts have broken down the process into stages similar to more general stages of policy decisions of all types.[33] The process typically begins with awareness of the innovation or detection of a problem that calls for action. In the latter case, search routines for seeking solutions will be invoked. Coalitions will form to support or oppose individual proposals, and a choice will ultimately be made. It may result in adoption of a new program or its defeat, although the latter outcome is not studied with great frequency.

If an innovation is adopted, it must then be implemented, a process that is often difficult and full of pitfalls, at least in the short run. The change is eventually evaluated, which may lead to its termination or continuation. In the latter case, it gradually comes to be part of the status quo, although revisions may follow. The overall process is considerably more complex than a simple choice of innovating or not.[34]

The emphasis on stages in the innovation process casts light on the many obstacles that face individual changes. They may not be noticed, or they may fail to attract sufficient support. The effort to translate the official policy into action may prove unsuccessful, or an evaluation of the results may be unfavorable. Innovations do not come easily.

A substantial body of the literature addresses the issue of influences on the adoption of innovations.[35] One concern centers on the characteristics of the changes themselves. Some require massive expenditures of funds for personnel, equipment, subsidies, and other necessities. Others are comparatively inexpensive. Some may be relatively compatible with existing systems and orientations, but others may require many drastic and painful changes. An innovation may involve complex, esoteric technology or may be comparatively simple to understand and execute. Innovations vary in terms of whether they can be tried on a limited, experimental basis rather than requiring a large commitment that will be very difficult to terminate. A change and its effects may be visible and dramatic or may be noticed by only a few people.[36]

The concern for the traits of innovations is linked to the view that innovativeness is not purely undimensional (although average innovativeness may still vary across individuals or governments). An organization, therefore, might be quick to adopt inexpensive changes but slow to adopt expensive ones. An individual who spurns a change that requires mastery of complex technical skills may quickly choose one that is technically simple. Propensities to innovate may therefore depend on the nature of the change.

Other influences on the adoption of innovations are at least partly separate from the nature of the changes. Reforms may be spurred by a problem — anything from a dramatic crisis to a vague sense that current programs are not performing well enough or as well as programs elsewhere.[37] Of course, problems may lead to paralysis and deadlock if decision makers do not manage the problems effectively.[38] Nonetheless, problems can often be a force for change.

The adoption of changes may also be shaped by the resource environment.[39] The availability of funds that are not needed for current operations, underutilized equipment, and skilled personnel facilitate searching for new proposals and adopting them, but resources may not be critical for comparatively inexpensive or technically simple innovations.[40]

Political forces may also shape innovation decisions. The presence of a general inclination to preserve past ways and traditional values is likely to discourage changes that could overturn or threaten established practices.[41] In addition, the political climate generally includes some sense of the appropriate scope of governmental activity and the values and priorities that government programs should follow. Changes consistent with the prevailing beliefs and values are more likely to be adopted than those that threaten those values.[42]

Innovation, then, has many facets, and researchers have taken numerous approaches in exploring the subject. Not surprisingly, findings have not always been consistent from one study to another. Nevertheless, a great deal has been learned in recent decades.

The States as Innovators

To some observers, studying innovation in the American states seems a rather futile task, akin to seeking peace and quiet on a gunnery range. Critics have complained that state governments are comparatively backward, rooted in tradition, slow to face problems, and reluctant to change or modernize.[43] According to Adrian, "At one time state governments were known as experimental laboratories in American democracy. . . . They have not recently been innovators."[44] As we will see shortly, not all observers share this perspective.

One of the strongest critics of state governments, Roscoe Martin, depicted the inclinations of state leaders in the following terms:

> What has been done over a period of years can continue to be done, but what is new and different must be regarded with suspicion. . . . [State leaders] mean to risk neither position nor power through entertainment of "radical" (that is, new or different) propositions. . . . Addiction to the status quo leads almost invariably to an unfavorable reaction to anything new or strange. . . . State leaders are by confession cautious and tradition-bound.[45]

While Martin acknowledged that not all state leaders fit that pattern, he contended that most did.

Some observers regard the states' reluctance to innovate (to the degree that such a characterization is accurate) as an outgrowth of the rural and small-town environments from which many state leaders were recruited. In rural areas and small towns, people tend to be insulated from the consequences of one another's actions by distance. Strong primary groups such as families, stable neighborhoods, and churches regulate individual behavior. People are shielded from the social problems and interdependence of large cities. Rural and small-town settings, then, tend to produce leaders who perceive little need for change, especially if the change involves an expansion of government activities.[46]

That mentality is graphically captured by a sampler in the office of a small-town official:

MAKE IT DO
WEAR IT OUT
USE IT UP
DO WITHOUT[47]

That frame of mind is hardly conducive to a vigorous search for new program options or the mobilization of support to enact those options and carry them to the implementation stage.

Not all observers accept the contention that the states are backwaters forever rooted in the past, at least not wholeheartedly. Sharkansky contends that the states have often been more creative and effective than is commonly recognized.[48] Not all policy innovations made headlines or received extensive coverage on the evening news. The image of backwardness may be misleading. Certainly the image of the states that emerged in the 1980s and 1990s is one of greater creativity and receptivity to change than in earlier times.

A major difficulty in determining whether the states are generally innovative or tradition-bound stems from the fact that different observers may have different expectations regarding a suitable level of innovativeness. In addition, the states vary considerably in the speed with which they adopt new programs.[49] Walker's analysis revealed that in the late 1800s an average of more than fifty years elapsed between the first adoption of an innovation and its last adoption. That time span decreased to approximately twenty-five years by the middle of the twentieth century.[50] The propensity to adopt innovations clearly varies from state to state. Generalizations regarding the slowness or backwardness of the slowest adopters may be inappropriate for the early adopters.

Further complications arise because states that are quick to adopt one type of policy reform, such as civil rights legislation, may not be quick to adopt reforms in other policy areas, such as law enforcement or health care.[51] Moreover, a state that is generally quick to do new things at one point in history may be slow to act at others.[52] The leader of today may be a laggard tomorrow.

Reaching general conclusions regarding the typical level of state innovations is therefore a difficult task, but the literature clearly indicates that significant innovative activity occurs in the states. In view of the many obstacles to policy innovation, the presence of any change may seem surprising.

Obstacles to Innovation

Under the best of circumstances, policy innovations face an imposing array of obstacles that taken together are successful in stopping many from being adopted. The obstacles are sufficiently numerous and powerful to give pause to many advocates of policy change. The fact that changes occur indicates that the barriers can be overcome, but success usually does not come easily.

An initial obstacle is the tendency for individuals and organizations to refrain from searching for a new approach or technique unless they

are noticeably dissatisfied with the current system.[53] If current performance levels are regarded as adequate, decision makers, who typically
have many tasks to perform, are likely to feel little inclination to seek
alternatives. Moreover, expectations regarding performance often come
to reflect current performance levels: if a program fails to perform at a
level that was previously expected, decision makers may gradually revise
their expectations downward.[54] Reasons for performance problems are
rarely difficult to find, and the result may be acceptance of a previously
unsatisfactory level of achievement.

Decision makers, then, are not necessarily looking for policy innovations. In an organization that already has a substantial work load
arising from current activities, little energy may be available for seeking
new approaches and programs, and potential reforms may languish.
They are not consciously rejected but simply ignored.

Cost considerations also deter many innovations.[55] The very act of
searching for new options is costly. Personnel must be allocated to the
search process; reference materials may be needed; and communication
with potential sources of ideas will probably be required.[56] The search
process is likely to be time-consuming as well. Amassing sufficient resources to search for potential innovations is difficult when those resources are also in demand for supporting operations.

Cost considerations also arise when organizations analyze potential
innovations to assess their suitability. Analysis is often costly, particularly when many options are analyzed, when the options have a variety
of consequences, and when program results are affected by a variety of
phenomena besides the program.[57] Hiring expert personnel, obtaining
precise measures of program results and costs, and establishing systems
for evaluating program options can be very expensive. Obtaining those
resources in the face of competing demands from current programs is
typically difficult.

Adoption of an innovation brings the prospect of additional costs.
Additional personnel may be needed if a change requires more workers
or workers with different skills. Alternatively, employees may need additional training, which is also costly. New equipment and facilities may be
required, or older ones may have to be substantially modified. Further
costs result.[58]

In a related vein, sunk costs of established program and practices
serve to deter innovations.[59] An existing program may have required
substantial investments in equipment, building, facilities, and supplies.
Expert staff members may have been hired or developed through training programs or work experience. Elected officials who oversee the programs have devoted time and energy to mastering those programs and

their operations. Change risks rendering those past investments useless. Overall, cost concerns are often a powerful deterrent to policy changes.

Fear of provoking conflict or criticism is yet another deterrent to policy innovation.[60] Major changes in programs or procedures may disrupt established relationships in public agencies. Administrators who previously exerted influence by virtue of their experience with the old system may find their importance diminished. Agencies that previously functioned in isolation from one another may be forced to work closely together. Past work habits may need to be changed, and employees may find retooling their work skills a stressful experience.[61] Not surprisingly, advocates of change are often seen as "breeders of trouble and conflict."[62]

Innovations also bring the risk of criticism and opposition from groups that benefit from existing arrangements and programs.[63] Agency personnel whose jobs may be eliminated or downgraded by an innovation can be expected to oppose it vigorously. They may also develop emotional bonds to an agency and its programs and consequently oppose efforts to eliminate or merge the agency or significantly alter its programs.[64]

Program clientele are often staunch defenders of the status quo.[65] Providers of agency supplies and material do not want innovations that would render those materials unnecessary. Paving contractors can be expected to oppose paring back road and highway programs to free resources for nonroad transportation programs. Recipients of services and benefits, whether subsidies, conveniences, legal advantages, or other things of value, are typically hostile to program changes that threaten those benefits. Organizations subject to public regulation may reach accommodations with regulatory agencies and consequently oppose innovations that might upset that accommodation. Fear of angering program clientele, then, undercuts many potential innovations.

Innovations may also provoke criticisms from elected officials, for a variety of reasons.[66] Some officials may disagree with the goals of a change or doubt its effectiveness. Long-standing, mutually rewarding relationships among elected officials, administrative agencies, and program clientele may be threatened by some innovations, a circumstance that will trigger opposition. Officials who supported adoption and continuation of existing programs and policies may be hesitant to adopt new approaches that reduce the value of past experience. Elected officials are not necessarily receptive to change, a circumstance that hampers policy reform.

Policymakers often fear the uncertainty major policy changes may bring.[67] A new initiative may cost much more than decision makers originally expected. A classic case is the social services grants program, the cost of which skyrocketed by more than 350 percent in only three years.[68] A policy provision that receives little attention may trigger unrest and political tension, as in the case of the community action programs. Their requirement for "maximum feasible participation" by the people served by the programs led to bitter struggles for control of some programs.[69]

The uncertainties associated with an innovation take a wide variety of forms. A new program may not be as effective as policymakers expected, or the program's benefits may emerge more slowly than anticipated. In either case, officials, who are often tempted to overstate the benefits of a proposal to increase its political palatability, will be in a difficult position. People may not react to a new program as decision makers expected, so that the program's effectiveness is undercut. Construction of a new freeway to relieve traffic congestion may encourage more construction in the area and more driving, so that congestion remains just as severe and possibly worse. New programs may produce indirect effects that create new problems. A new anticrime program in one area may cause criminal activity to shift to other areas, which in turn experience an increase in crime. Because dramatic policy changes bring considerable uncertainty, officials often prefer the relative predictability of current programs to the unknown risks of innovation.[70]

Innovation is further discouraged by the obstacle course new proposals must overcome to become law.[71] A new initiative may be defeated in a legislative committee, in a legislative floor vote, in a disagreement between house and senate (except in Nebraska, which has a unicameral legislature), or by a gubernatorial veto (except in North Carolina, where the governor has no veto power). The state political parties, which might help to bridge the gaps between institutions, are the victims of a painful dilemma. States where one party is much larger than the other typically find that the larger party is relatively successful in electing its members to all branches. However, the dominant party in a one-party state tends to be poorly organized and fragmented, so that although the party may have nominal control of all policy-making branches, it is likely to be too weak to coordinate their activities. The parties in a competitive setting tend to be better organized and more cohesive,[72] but neither party is likely to gain control of all branches simultaneously.[73]

Because enacting policy change is typically so difficult, with many points at which new initiatives can be defeated, the advantages of the status quo are generally very strong. Indeed, the difficulty of enacting policy changes may deter officials from even proposing innovations. A governor or legislative leader who initiates a proposal that is subsequently defeated may suffer a loss of prestige and credibility.[74] The difficulty of pushing major changes through the legislative process creates powerful incentives for choosing minor adjustments to current programs rather than innovations.

On balance, then, while the literature may at times be guilty of a bias in favor of innovations,[75] they often carry significant liabilities. Searching for innovative proposals and carrying them out can be costly. A new policy brings uncertainty and may generate major political conflict. Previous investments in skills and equipment may be rendered irrelevant by a new policy. An effort to adopt a reform may fail and damage the reputations of its proponents; conversely, the price of adoption may be the alienation of other decision makers or groups or the accumulation of political debts that weigh heavily on the proponents of the reform in the future. If state officials often prefer to adhere closely to past practices, that inclination is not irrational. The following analysis therefore does not assume that innovation is necessarily good or bad. As with other types of policy decisions, the virtues and shortcomings of a particular change may be in the eye of the beholder.

The Plan of the Book

Chapter 2 will develop a framework for explaining why innovations are adopted in some cases but not others. The framework will be presented in general terms flexible enough to accommodate a broad variety of innovations. Subsequent chapters will apply that framework to a number of policy changes, from teacher competency testing and state-financed property tax relief programs to sunset legislation and public ownership of railroads.

The innovations do not constitute a random sample of state policy decisions. They do, however, span much of the responsibility of state governments. Education, transportation, government finance, criminal justice, and election laws are all represented in the analysis. Some of the innovations entail direct costs, but others do not. Some have been matters of considerable public controversy; others have attracted little public attention.

The concluding chapter will assess the performance of the different explanations for policy innovation across various innovations. It will seek to determine what types of change are likely to be encouraged or discouraged by the problem environment, the availability of resources, and orientations regarding the use of government power. Some tentative generalizations regarding the sorts of innovations shaped by various influences will be offered.

NOTES

See Bibliography for full reference.

1. Thoreau (1976: 288).
2. Kaufman (1976).
3. Sharkansky (1968: chapters 3–4); but see also Dye (1984: 248–249).
4. Walker (1969: 881).
5. March and Simon (1958: 174–175).
6. See also Agnew (1980: 7); Downs (1976: xv); Gray (1973: 1174); Thompson (1969: 5).
7. Mohr (1969: 112).
8. Mohr (1969: 112; emphasis added); see also Lineberry (1978: 62–66); Polsby (1984: 8).
9. See Edelman (1964).
10. For overviews of that field, see Gramlich (1981) and Mohr (1988).
11. Zaltman, Duncan, and Holbek (1973: 10); see also Rogers (1983: 11).
12. Wildavsky (1974: 115).
13. Bingham (1976: 4).
14. Walker (1969: 895).
15. Of course, a merit system requires mechanisms for assessing skills, but a well-administered patronage system requires analogous mechanisms for monitoring political contributions and activities.
16. For broad overviews and bibliographies, see Rogers (1983); Zaltman, Duncan, and Holbek (1973); Savage (1985).
17. Rogers (1983: chapter 5); Savage (1985: 2–3).
18. Rogers (1983: chapter 10); Savage (1985: 2–3); Thompson (1969); Zaltman, Duncan, and Holbek (1973).
19. Bingham (1976); Gray (1973); Polsby (1984); Savage (1978); Walker (1969).
20. Eyestone (1977); Gray (1973).
21. Rogers (1983: chapter 9).
22. Kingdon (1984: 188–193).
23. Savage (1985: 4–5, 10–11).
24. Rogers (1983: chapter 7); Savage (1978); Walker (1969).
25. Eyestone (1977); Gray (1973).
26. Savage (1978); Gray (1973).
27. Gray (1973).
28. Savage (1978).
29. Gray (1973: 1176).
30. Eyestone (1977).
31. Walker (1969: 892–894).
32. Walker (1969: 896).
33. On the concept of policy stages, see Anderson (1984: chapters 3, 4, 6); Dye (1984: chapters 13–14); Jones (1984: chapters 4–6, 8–9); Peters (1986: chapters 3–5, 7).
34. Rogers (1983: 15–16; chapter 6); Zaltman, Duncan, and Holbek (1973: 33–38).
35. Agnew (1980: 7).

36. Rogers (1983: 15–16, chapter 6); Zaltman, Duncan, and Holbek (1973: 33–38).

37. Barnett (1953: 167); Cyert and March (1963: 120–121, 278); Downs (1967); Eyestone (1977: 446–447).

38. Polsby (1984: 170–171).

39. Bingham (1976: 7–8); Downs (1976: 48); Downs and Mohr (1980: 90); Walker (1969: 883).

40. Downs (1976: 95–97); Savage (1985: 12).

41. Bingham (1976: 7–8); Mohr (1969: 112–113).

42. Rogers (1983: 15); Zaltman, Duncan, and Holbek (1973: 37–38).

43. For cautious reviews of those criticisms, see Sanford (1967: 1–5); Sharkansky (1978: 2–7).

44. Adrian (1976: 56).

45. Martin (1965: 78–79).

46. Adrian (1976: 42–43); Adrian and Press (1977: 15–16, 26–27).

47. The sampler is mentioned in Shulman (1954) and quoted in Adrian and Press (1977: 28).

48. Sharkansky (1978).

49. Walker (1969); Savage (1978).

50. Walker (1969: 895).

51. Gray (1973); Savage (1985: 10–11).

52. Savage (1978).

53. Downs (1967: 169); March and Simon (1958: 173–174).

54. March and Simon (1958: 182).

55. Brewer and deLeon (1983: 64).

56. Downs (1967: 168).

57. March and Simon (1958: 173); Lindblom (1959).

58. Mohr (1969: 114).

59. Dye (1987: 36–37); Edwards and Sharkansky (1978: 250–251); March and Simon (1958: 173).

60. Dye (1987: 37); Lindblom (1959); Lineberry (1978: 34–35).

61. Brewer and deLeon (1983: 283–284).

62. Downs (1967: 275).

63. Brewer and deLeon (1983: 288).

64. Edwards and Sharkansky (1978: 280–281); Kaufman (1976: 9–10).

65. Kaufman (1976: 10–11); Peters (1986: 21); Wildavsky (1974: 13–14).

66. Kaufman, 1976: 5–6.

67. Dye (1987: 36); Lindblom (1959); Thompson (1969: 6).

68. Derthick (1975: 2).

69. Moynihan (1970); Sundquist and Davis (1969: chapter 2).

70. See also Mohr (1969: 114); Walker (1969: 890); Walker (1971: 385).

71. Kaufman (1976: 3–5); Peters (1986: 20–21).

72. Nice (1979: chapter 2).

73. Ranney (1976: 81–82).

74. For supportive evidence, see Ostrom and Simon (1985: 350–351).

75. For a discussion of that issue, see Rogers (1983: 92–94).

A Model of
Policy Innovation

Introduction

In view of the many obstacles to the adoption of policy innovations, we might expect state governments to continue doing approximately the same things decade after decade. Continuity is indeed a major feature in state politics,[1] but states do break from the past and embark on new courses of action.[2] A major focus for innovation researchers is explaining why innovations are adopted.

The immensity of the innovation literature, coupled with the variety of disciplines involved in innovation research and the diversity of subjects analyzed, from individuals to corporations, social clubs, and governments, have produced a large number of different formulations to explain innovation decisions. This chapter will develop a relatively broad model of governmental innovation, a model that draws on the insights produced by numerous scholars, including those who study nongovernmental change. Other literature on policy-making in general will flesh out the model and contribute additional perspectives.

The model that will form the basis for later analyses contains three components. First, the problem environment may stimulate adoption. Officials' inclinations to search for and adopt a new approach may reflect whether it can solve or ameliorate a serious problem. Second, the availability of resources may encourage innovation. Innovations are often costly, and officials in states amply endowed with financial and other resources can meet those costs more easily. Third, orientations toward governmental activity and change may encourage or discourage innovation. Where the past is revered and government is viewed with skepticism or even hostility, adopting new governmental programs is likely to be difficult. In addition, a reform that is not compatible with prevailing values faces an uphill struggle. I will examine each component of the model in turn.

The Problem Environment

Researchers have long regarded the problem environment as a significant influence on the adoption of innovations, at least in some cases.[3] Problems shape many policy decisions, innovative and noninnovative,[4] but many researchers have placed considerable emphasis on problems as sources of innovation. The problems are not all of the same variety, however.

Some analysts place particular emphasis on the role of dramatic crises or conspicuous failures in stimulating change.[5] A world war may spur the development of new weapons and military tactics. The assassination of a public figure may foster adoption of new security arrangements or gun-control laws. An interruption in the flow of oil imports may trigger enactment of programs designed to encourage energy independence, at least for a time.[6]

Not all problems constitute crises, but problems that are not crises may still encourage policy changes. A gap between the state of affairs people expect and actual conditions may lead decision makers to conclude that a new approach is needed.[7] Several factors may produce a gap between expectations and results. Conditions may grow worse as a problem becomes more severe or the current policies designed to solve it lose effectiveness. Expectations regarding a suitable level of program performance may change as cultural values change or people learn that related programs in other states or countries are more effective.

The perception of a gap does not necessarily correspond closely to how well a program performs.[8] An isolated incident may heighten concerns regarding crime or the safety of air travel, regardless of whether the overall crime rate or air safety has changed noticeably. Conversely, a problem may quietly grow worse without the changing conditions being recognized.

The problem environment influences innovation in a number of ways. First, a severe problem, particularly if it is regarded as a crisis, may serve to force decision makers to pay attention to an issue.[9] Innovation rarely occurs until an issue receives serious attention, and decision makers rarely if ever have time to consider all issues.

Problems, dramatic or not, also spur innovation by encouraging decision makers to search for new and better ways of doing things. When people are relatively satisfied with a program's performance, they may feel little need to seek alternatives to that program. Other tasks will typically be clamoring for attention; little time or energy may be available for identifying changes unless a problem goads policymakers into looking for them.[10]

In addition to increasing awareness of issues and stimulating searches for new options, problems may foster innovation at the choice phase of policy-making. As noted earlier, policymakers are often reluctant to try new approaches. In the words of Robert Lineberry: "Left to its own devices, the political system would probably operate incrementally, churning out next year's policy as a carbon copy of last year's policy, plus a little."[11] That reluctance regarding major changes, while often criticized, is not entirely without merit.

The problem environment can alter the common preference for the familiar at the choice stage in a number of ways. Decision makers may decide on their own that a crisis or deteriorating situation calls for bolder action than a modest increase in current programs can provide. The prospects for innovation are consequently improved. Problems may bring demands from the public and interest groups for drastic measures or at least substantially improved performance.[12] Those demands may convince decision makers that the risks of innovating are outweighed by the risks associated with not meeting the demands.

A perception of serious problems may also cause an innovation to be imposed on an organization from the outside.[13] Not all changes are chosen in a wholly voluntary fashion. State adoption of the 55 MPH speed limit was spurred by a requirement attached to federal highway aid. A state mandate may require local governments to provide a service they would not have adopted otherwise. The degree of coercion or inducement can take a wide variety of forms, from financial incentives and legal sanctions to the use of military occupation, as in the governmental changes in Germany and Japan following World War II and Reconstruction in the American South after the Civil War.

Overall, the problem-environment perspective indicates that innovation is likely to follow the development of a problem, particularly if it is regarded as a crisis. More severe and dramatic problems provide greater stimulus for innovation, while satisfactory program performance is likely to encourage continuation of the status quo. In this view, officials are not likely to incur the costs and risks associated with innovation if things seem to be going well. Proponents of change in that context are likely to encounter responses of "Don't rock the boat" and "If it ain't broke, don't fix it." Not until a problem has arisen and reached painful proportions are the advocates of change likely to receive a cordial reception.

According to the problem-environment perspective, then, adoptions of specific policy innovations are more likely in states with more serious problems in the task environments that those innovations seek to address. In states where a problem is less severe, change regarding that problem is less likely.

A NOTE OF CAUTION. Although the hypothesis that problems or crises foster innovation seems quite obvious, researchers have long recognized that there are many potential slippages between the problem environment and policy decisions. Studies have been able to explain some policy decisions with a high degree of accuracy with little or no reference to the problem environment.[14] Taken together, the obstacles to a direct link between problems and policy responses are formidable.

At the outset, public officials do not notice all the problems facing society.[15] Some problems are ignored as the result of conscious decisions, but others are simply missed, for a variety of reasons. Noticing problems is far from automatic.

Some problems are overlooked because the methods for detecting and measuring them are faulty.[16] Certain types of pollution were difficult to detect for many years, a circumstance that contributed to neglect. Crimes that are not reported typically lead to the assumption (by officials) that those crimes do not occur. Foreign powers may develop new military capabilities or begin to provide covert aid to an insurgent movement in another country, but detecting those changes is a difficult task; if they are successfully concealed, as the foreign powers often try to do, an appropriate response may not be forthcoming.

Other problems are overlooked because officials can think about a limited number of matters at one time. There are typically hundreds of problems clamoring for attention; as a result, some issues are pushed aside by the sheer volume of other issues.[17] And that competition for attention is far from neutral. Matters that are already recognized governmental responsibilities consume much of the agenda space. New problems that have previously not been regarded as governmental concerns are generally at a serious disadvantage in competing for agenda space with established public responsibilities.[18]

Some problems are not addressed because of a conscious decision not to give them serious attention, even though they are recognized. Citizens may lack confidence in the government's ability to solve a problem and therefore conclude that they do not wish to devote the time and energy needed to bring the problem to the attention of public officials.

Alternatively, the officials may notice a problem but not know how to deal with it. Because officials are typically reluctant to devote considerable attention to a problem if the probable outcome is a public admission of helplessness, problems that lack known solutions are likely to be shunted aside.[19]

Other concerns regarding the consequences of a public airing of an issue may discourage giving it attention. Choosing problems to consider may have implications for public officials' careers; they are inclined to avoid problems that threaten their careers.[20] An issue may divide a governor's coalition, cast a spotlight on past actions that policymakers would prefer to forget, or provide a launching pad for challengers in future elections.

Officials may also fear that raising an issue will set uncontrollable forces in motion and ultimately lead to a policy change the officials regard as undesirable. Broadening the scope of a conflict can alter the balance of power and lead to results different from the probable outcome if the conflict had remained relatively private.[21] Officials may therefore notice a problem but refrain from giving it public recognition in order to prevent some groups from exerting influence. A variety of tactics, including delays, threats, and emphasizing other issues, can be used to prevent an issue from becoming visible.[22]

The public and officials may recognize a problem but regard it as beyond the realm of governmental responsibilities. Mass and elite perceptions regarding the role of government encourage public involvement in resolving some problems and discourage public action on other problems.[23] Views of the proper scope of governmental activity may vary from place to place; that variation will in turn encourage action where the role of government is viewed broadly and discourage recognition of equally severe problems where the government's role is narrowly defined.

Even if a problem is noticed and regarded as a public responsibility, the result may not be policy innovation. As noted earlier, the obstacle course that all legislation must pass through is filled with opportunities for defeating initiatives.[24] Officials may decide that the best response to a problem is increased funding for existing programs or more personnel carrying out long-standing activities rather than trying anything new. Conversely, officials may recognize a problem and regard it as a public responsibility but decide to do nothing. They may lack the resources to attack the problem; they may not know how to respond. The weight of previous commitments may be too great to permit new initiatives. Officials may postpone action in the hope that the problem will correct itself or be resolved by another level of government. A severe crisis may induce panic and produce fumbling or paralysis rather than innovation.[25]

Overall, there are many possibilities for slippage between the nature of the problem environment and the adoption of policy innovations. While problems may serve to stimulate innovation in some cases, then, the connection is far from automatic or dependable. A number of factors other than the problem environment may play a role in the adoption or defeat of innovations.

Resources

A number of studies have found that resources, particularly economic resources, help to explain a wide variety of policy outcomes, from welfare benefit levels to legal representation for the poor.[26] According to the slack innovation perspective, the availability of resources not needed for ongoing operations is a powerful force for innovation. If all available resources are needed to meet current commitments, innovation is not likely to occur.[27]

Slack resources encourage innovation in a variety of ways. The process of searching for new approaches or programs requires personnel, information, and appropriate facilities, all of which are costly. Analyzing potential innovations generates additional costs, particularly if the contemplated changes are large and require adjustments in other programs. The adoption of new programs may require new personnel or the retraining of current staff, new equipment, and new facilities. Organizations with ample resources can meet those costs more easily.[28]

Slack resources also encourage innovation because of the uncertainty change brings. Officials in a state straining to meet the costs of current programs may be reluctant to expend scarce resources on a new approach that may ultimately fail, a result likely to produce complaints that the resources were wasted. Moreover, the failure may cause damage and therefore generate additional costs. Slack resources make those uncertain costs easier to absorb and help encourage innovation.[29]

Slack resources may foster innovation to avoid "the embarrassment of unused resources."[30] An agency, public or private, has powerful incentives to spend virtually all the funds allocated to it by higher authorities. An agency with large numbers of idle personnel or a large budgetary surplus is typically vulnerable to the charge that it has more resources than it needs and should be pared back.[31] Devoting those otherwise idle resources to searching for innovations and analyzing them provides a justification for the continuing availability of those resources, as does the cost of putting reforms into practice. The result of these activities is likely to be increased innovation.

The prosperity of a state is a critical aspect of the resource environment. Because states compete with one another for jobs, investment, and affluent citizens, officials fear that raising tax rates much higher than the rates of other states will be harmful to the state's prospects for economic growth.[32] As a result, officials in affluent states find that raising revenues is considerably easier than in poorer states. In that context, wealthier states have an obvious advantage in generating slack resources needed for innovation.

Urbanization is in some respects another aspect of the resource environment, although urbanization has other components as well. The creative resources of a state are likely to be found in its urban and metropolitan areas.[33] Centers of advanced learning and research, as well as organizations large enough to permit specialization, tend to be concentrated in urban and metropolitan settings. Rural states may have a more difficult time amassing the skill resources needed for innovation.

Urbanization may also spur demands for reform because of the nature of urban life. In rural and small-town settings, people are somewhat insulated from one another's actions by distance. A network of relatively strong primary groups, including families, churches, and neighborhoods, serves to regulate behavior. In urban and metropolitan areas, physical proximity causes people to be more affected by one another's actions. Primary groups are less effective in controlling behavior, and interactions tend to be impersonal. Metropolitan areas also attract people seeking a better life; their expectations may exceed what the social, economic, and political systems can provide.[34] Metropolitan settings, then, are likely to create more pressures for governmental innovation as a method of coping with the interdependence, weakened social controls, and frustrated expectations associated with metropolitan life.

A NOTE OF WARNING. Slack resources are not always helpful in accounting for policy innovations.[35] Just as individual lifestyles vary in ways that cannot be explained by affluence, state policy changes are not always a reflection of the resource environment.

Resources may be less important for innovations that are comparatively inexpensive. While searching for some innovations can be costly and time-consuming, other proposals are widely publicized and well known. Associations of public officials, the media, and interest groups disseminate information about proposals on a regular basis. In a similar vein, although some potential changes require costly and difficult research to assess their costs and benefits, other proposals are comparatively simple to analyze and require little elaborate, costly research. Not all innovations call for new equipment, additional personnel, or vast outlays of funds. Slack resources may not be necessary for innovations that are widely known, require little analysis, and are inexpensive to put into practice.[36]

The inclinations of policymakers may also determine whether resources will be used to adopt innovations.[37] Resources may be abundantly available, but if a particular innovation is not regarded as necessary or useful, its prospects for adoption may be slim. Conversely, if officials believe that a problem is so serious that some form of response is unavoidable, the result may be innovation, even if resources are difficult to come by. Indeed, some innovations can even produce revenues: Mississippi, one of the poorest states in the country, has been a national leader in the adoption of the general sales tax and local government financing of industrial development.[38]

Officials who have abundant resources may decide to provide more generous funding for ongoing programs, a decision that is likely to be pleasing to the beneficiaries of those programs. Note too that abundant resources in a state may or may not mean abundant resources in state government. State officials may decide that wealth should remain in the private sector or local governments rather than being devoted to state policy innovations. A particular change, then, may be crowded aside by other concerns, public or private. A complete model of policy innovation must consider the political currents that move through the policymaking process as well as the problem environment facing officials and the availability of resources.

Orientations Regarding Government Power and Change

While innovations may reflect the problem environment and the availability of slack resources, orientations toward the use of government power and change may also influence adoption of innovations. Those orientations include the views of the public, the inclinations of the political parties, and accumulated experience with policy change. Not all the various aspects are likely to be relevant in all situations, but one or more aspects may be.

The broad climate of public opinion is likely to shape innovative behavior in several respects. First, public views regarding the appropriate scope of government activity and the proper goals of government will shape which issues are brought to the attention of public officials.[39] Where governmental responsibilities are viewed broadly, more issues will fall within government's domain, and policy innovations involving these issues are less likely to remain in the background.

The opinion climate may also influence the process of searching for policy options. Where people view bold changes skeptically, officials are more likely to confine their attention to proposals that closely resemble current policies. In a related vein, the opinion climate in some states may be more tolerant of the adoption of new approaches and techniques. Public sentiment elsewhere may discourage enactment of substantial policy changes.[40]

In addition to general views regarding activism and change, the degree of compatibility between a specific change and the prevailing opinion climate may shape that change's prospects for adoption.[41] People may be wary of change in general but regard a particular innovation as likely to achieve a cherished goal and consequently support that innovation enthusiastically. Conversely, people may be generally receptive to change but conclude that a specific innovation is a threat to the achievement of key objectives and defend the status quo. Note that this possibility echoes the previous discussion regarding innovation as at least partially issue-specific: receptivity depends on the nature of the innovation.

The ideological leanings of the public, according to this view, may shape the prospects for innovation in two ways. First, in general terms, liberalism is likely to encourage policy innovation. Because liberals tend to believe in a broader role for government, a liberal opinion climate is likely to bring more issues to the attention of policymakers. In addition, liberals tend to have more faith in analysis and to be more open to experimentation and change. Conservatism, with its skepticism of social analysis and experimentation and greater belief in traditional values and practices, is likely to provide a less receptive climate for innovation.[42]

A second linkage between ideology and innovation, however, is based on the compatibility of specific innovations and the general opinion climate. Ideological conservatism tends to favor the market as a mechanism for allocating resources.[43] A conservative opinion climate, in this view, is likely to encourage adoption of reforms that protect or extend the role of market allocation. In a similar fashion, although conservatives are generally skeptical regarding government activism, they may support the use of public authority to support traditional values and patterns of behavior.[44] Innovations consistent with those goals may receive a warm reception in conservative opinion climates. By contrast, liberalism's emphasis on equality[45] is likely to mean a positive reaction to reforms that promote equality and a hostile reaction to re-

forms fostering inequality in states with comparatively liberal electorates.

The study of public opinion in the states has been hamstrung by the
immense costs of the sample size that would be needed to achieve reasonably precise estimates. Robert Erikson solved that problem by using
polls conducted during the 1930s.[46] The samples used in a few polls
conducted in that era were large enough to provide estimates of opinions
in individual states. Other researchers have utilized simulation techniques to estimate state public opinion from national opinion surveys
and each state's regional and demographic characteristics.[47] A potential
problem with the simulation approach, however, stems from the possibility that a single state may have a distinctive opinion climate that
cannot be explained by national opinion patterns and the state's regional
and demographic traits.

The ideological leanings of state electorates are indicated with considerable precision by the division of the two-party presidential vote in
1972. Election studies indicate that ideological and issue concerns
strongly influenced individual voting decisions in that election and that
party loyalties were less influential than in other presidential elections.[48]
Moreover, voting patterns by congressional districts in the 1972 presidential race were strongly associated with the liberalism of members of
Congress in floor votes.[49] States with more liberal electorates, as indicated by the McGovern vote, tend to have more liberal public policies.[50]

A more recent estimate of state opinion has been developed by
Wright, Erikson, and McIver.[51] By combining a large number of surveys
conducted from 1974 through 1982, they were able to obtain reasonably
precise estimates of the ideological self-identification of state electorates.
Their estimates are the most direct evidence on state opinion and are
related to state policy liberalism.[52]

A very different measure of the state opinion climate involves classi-
fying the states according to their dominant political cultures.[53] The
"cultures" go beyond views of the scope of appropriate government activity to include more specific concerns, such as emphasis on honesty in
government and hierarchical control. Although Elazar's classification is
impressionistic and therefore not as useful for indicating preferences
regarding government activism as the measures noted above, his measure is associated with a variety of state phenomena in ways that generally confirm its validity.[54]

Ideological currents may move through the political parties as well
as the electorate. Party ideologies influence the perceptions of decision
makers, their priorities, and their willingness to take risks on behalf of
particular proposals.[55] Party ideologies may reflect the types of people

who support a party and the people likely to join a party. Ideological positions, then, reflect the coalitional bases of the parties and the potential supporters the parties seek to attract.[56] A variety of studies have found relationships between party ideologies and coalitional bases and policy outcomes, both nationally and at the state level.[57]

Two general strategies for measuring state party ideologies have been used. One approach utilizes ideological ratings of state party delegations to the U.S. House and Senate.[58] A basic problem with the strategy arises from states that have small to nonexistent congressional delegations of one party or the other. If a state has no Republican U.S. senators or representatives, the ideology of that state's Republican party cannot be assessed through this strategy. If a state sends only one or two Democrats to Congress, that state's Democratic party will be classified based on the behavior of one or two people; their individual eccentricities may give a misleading picture of the state party.

A second, preferable strategy for assessing state party ideologies is based on voting records of state party delegations to the presidential nominating conventions. Although presidential nominating contests appear to be the epitome of candidate-centered politics, research on voting by state party delegations to the conventions reveals a stable pattern of ideological alignments.[59] Some state parties consistently support conservative candidates, and other state party delegations just as consistently back liberals. Still other state party delegations occupy a more moderate position and avoid candidates of either extreme. State party ideology measures based on national convention voting patterns are associated with a variety of state policy decisions.[60]

One other aspect of orientations toward change is previous experience with innovation in general. The states vary considerably in the average speed with which they have adopted new programs in the past.[61] Moreover, a number of studies have found that governments develop varying policy orientations. Once those orientations develop, they tend to persist and to shape subsequent policy decisions.[62] Past decisions often serve as guides to officials when they confront a new problem. In Walker's words, "Look for an analogy between the situation you are dealing with and some other situation . . . where the problem has been successfully resolved."[63]

Officials and citizens in states that are often quick to adopt new programs are likely to become more accustomed to policy changes. Subsequent changes are likely to be less upsetting in that context. People may take pride in being national leaders; further innovations may be expected to continue that leadership role.[64]

In states generally slow to adopt new programs, the virtue of patience is likely to gain added respectability. Policies that continue for decade after decade may come to be regarded as part of the natural order of things. Defending the status quo may become the expected practice for decision makers. Change, by virtue of its rarity, becomes alien and threatening. If people in some states take pride in being pioneers, others may take equal pride in preserving traditional ways and not being swayed by the latest political fad.

A NOTE OF SKEPTICISM. A number of considerations suggest that broad orientations toward government activism and change may not necessarily influence adoption of individual innovations. Some grounds for skepticism are relatively specific to state politics, but other concerns are more broadly based. Overall, there are many potential sources of slippage between broad political currents and specific policy decisions.

Regarding public opinion, a number of studies have questioned whether much of the public actually thinks in an ideological or consistent fashion.[65] Although ideological thinking has grown more common since the 1950s,[66] it remains a stranger to tens of millions. The signals that citizens send to government do not necessarily form a clear pattern.

The influence of the broad opinion climate is further restricted by the limited attention many people pay to state politics.[67] As state governments grow larger and more complex and the issues they face grow increasingly technical, citizens who pay only modest attention to state government are at an increasing disadvantage in trying to influence policy decisions.[68]

Even if citizens have consistent opinions and are reasonably well informed, they may fail to communicate their views clearly to public officials. People who abstain from political activity may not communicate their views to officials at all. Nor are officials always receptive to public views, particularly if those views challenge officials' cherished beliefs or are held by people whose backgrounds are different from those of policymakers.[69] The broad climate of opinion may therefore have little impact on policy decisions.

Skepticism regarding the policy-making role of the parties also abounds. A party's candidates and officeholders may discover that the only way to build a coalition large enough to win is to appeal to people with a wide variety of opinions. Party positions that are seen as obstacles to attracting supporters are downplayed, ignored, or even contradicted.[70] The diversity of views within each party, the dispersal of power within the parties, and the tendency for officials to prize their careers more highly than the party program all make firm party control over policies difficult.[71] The parties also confront many rivals in the policy-making process, particularly interest groups and public agencies. Their activities may undercut party influence, although there are numerous exceptions.[72]

A number of analysts have found evidence of weakening in the American political parties. Voter loyalties to the parties declined substantially from the 1950s through the early 1970s.[73] Party organizations have considerable difficulty controlling the nominating process, and new campaign technologies enable candidates to run for office independently of the party organizations.[74] The parties cannot easily assemble a team of candidates who support a common program and provide a stable base of popular support for those candidates. Party influence on policy decisions is problematic at best.[75]

There are also grounds for skepticism regarding the linkage between overall tendencies regarding innovativeness in the past and subsequent policy innovations. As noted earlier, propensities to adopt changes may depend on the type of change. States that are quick to adopt transportation innovations, for example, may not be similarly inclined to adopt administrative or welfare innovations.[76] States that have been relatively innovative in the past may respond to subsequent potential innovations in a wide variety of ways, depending on the subject matter of each proposal.

Further slippages may arise because even broad tendencies regarding innovation can change; a state may be a pioneer in one era but comparatively slow to act in a later era.[77] An extended period of inaction or slowness in responding to problems may lead to an accumulation of demands and unmet needs, and the resulting pressures may lead to a burst of innovations. By contrast, an extended period of innovative activity may exhaust policymakers and the public. The stresses, strains, and costs of a series of innovations in one era may lead to a period of relative caution and stability later.[78] The past is not always a model for the future.

Overall, then, there is ample reason for caution in expecting public sentiments, party ideology, or past innovativeness to influence later innovations. There are many slippages between the political winds that make headlines and the nitty-gritty of specific government decisions.

Summary

Although inertia is a powerful force in government much of the time, officials do manage to shake off the frequent preference for the familiar. Scholars have devoted substantial attention to the question of why innovation occurs and have cast considerable light on the issue. Formulations vary considerably from study to study, however, and the findings are diverse.

Some studies emphasize the role of problems in fostering innovation. A crisis, a deteriorating situation, or a vague perception that current performance is not satisfactory can spur decision makers into searching for new approaches, assessing their merits, and adopting those innovations that offer some prospect for improving the situation. In this view, officials are not normally inclined to bear the costs and risks associated with changes unless prodded into action by some sort of problem. More dramatic problems will yield more dramatic innovations.

Other analyses indicate that reforms are a function of abundant resources. If current programs and commitments, many of whose beneficiaries are working to ensure the continuation of those commitments, fully consume available resources, decision makers may be unable to afford the costs of searching for new proposals, analyzing them, and putting them into practice. Abundant resources make the costs of innovation easier to bear; moreover, innovation may provide a plausible use for resources that might otherwise be idle and therefore reduce the risk that they will be taken away.

A third perspective emphasizes orientations toward change and the use of public power and authority in encouraging or discouraging innovations. Skepticism regarding change and a lack of experience with policy changes are likely to discourage innovations. However, individual proposals that are likely to reach valued goals may win rapid adoption, even in jurisdictions where people are generally reluctant to change. Mass and elite perspectives regarding governmental power and change, then, may play pivotal roles in shaping innovation decisions.

The chapters that follow will assess the utility of these explanations in accounting for a number of state policy innovations. Some adaptations will be needed because of variations in the periods when different innovations began, their visibility, and the problem environments relevant to different innovations.

NOTES

See Bibliography for full reference.

1. For example, Hofferbert and Urice (1985); Sharkansky (1968: chapters 3–4).
2. Savage (1978); Walker (1969).
3. Eyestone (1977: 445–447).
4. For example, Worden and Worden (1986).
5. Cyert and March (1963: 120–121, 287); Edwards and Sharkansky (1978: 280–282); Polsby (1984: 168–169); Sharkansky (1970: 174–178).

6. Dye (1984: 181–192).

7. Barnett (1953: 167); Bingham (1976: 11–13); Downs (1967: 275); March and Simon (1958: 183).

8. Downs (1976: 103–105); Lineberry (1978: 63).

9. Edwards and Sharkansky (1978: 104–105).

10. See Cyert and March (1963: 120–121, 278); Downs (1967: 169); March and Simon (1958: 173–174).

11. Lineberry (1978: 61).

12. Edwards and Sharkansky (1978; 280–282).

13. Hall (1977: 293); Zaltman, Duncan, and Holbek (1973: 80).

14. For examples, see Crecine (1969); Wildavsky (1986: chapter 3).

15. Walker (1971: 335).

16. See Edwards and Sharkansky (1978: 90–99).

17. See Cobb and Elder (1972: 45); Crenson (1971: 159–165); Schattschneider (1960: 65).

18. Edwards and Sharkansky (1978: 101); Peters (1986: 47).

19. Edwards and Sharkansky (1978: 90, 109); Peters (1986: 47).

20. Anderson (1984: 51).

21. Schattschneider (1960).

22. See Bachratz and Baratz (1970: 44, 57); Crenson (1971: 180–181); Edwards and Sharkansky (1978: 107–109).

23. Anderson (1984: 51); Cobb and Elder (1972: 107–109); Edwards and Sharkansky (1978: 88–89).

24. Kaufman (1976: 3–5); Peters (1986: 20–21).

25. Polsby (1984: 170–171).

26. See Dye (1966); Dye (1987: 307–308, 343); Worden and Worden (1986).

27. Cyert and March (1963: 278–279); Rogers (1983: 248–252); Sharkansky (1970: 182–183); Zaltman, Duncan, and Holbek (1973: 17–18).

28. Downs and Mohr (1980: 90); March and Simon (1958: 173, 186–187); Walker (1969: 883).

29. Thompson (1969: 6, 42); Walker (1969: 883).

30. Thompson (1969: 42).

31. See Wildavsky (1974: 31).

32. Walker (1971: 366).

33. Walker (1969: 883).

34. Adrian (1976: 42–43); Adrian and Press (1977: 15–16, 26–27); Bardo and Hartman (1982: 101–102, 129–130, 198–199).

35. Fleischmann and Nice (1988); Savage (1985: 12).

36. Downs (1976: 63, 95–97); Downs and Mohr (1980: 77, 84); Zaltman, Duncan, and Holbek (1973: 33–35).

37. Bingham (1976: 10).

38. Walker (1971: 358).

39. Anderson (1984: 51); Cobb and Elder (1972: 93).

40. Bingham (1976: 7–8); Edwards and Sharkansky (1978: 234–236); Mohr (1969: 112–117).

41. Rogers (1983: 223–226); Zaltman, Duncan, and Holbek (1973: 37–38, 64–66).

42. On liberal and conservative beliefs, see Dolbeare and Dolbeare (1976: 56–69); Sargent (1981: 65–70); Sibley (1970: 501, 509–512).

43. Dolbeare and Dolbeare (1976: 57–58).

44. Sargent (1981: 66–67).

45. Dolbeare and Dolbeare (1976: 45–46).
46. Erikson (1976).
47. Hopkins (1974); Sutton (1973); Weber and Shaffer (1972).
48. DeClercq, Hurley, and Luttbeg (1981); Nie, Verba, and Petrocik (1976: 171–172).
49. Schwarz and Fenmore (1977).
50. Klingman and Lammers (1984); Nice (1983a).
51. Wright, Erikson, and McIver (1985).
52. Wright, Erikson, and McIver (1987).
53. Elazar (1972: 94–102, 118).
54. See Klingman and Lammers (1984); Nice (1983b); Sharkansky (1969).
55. Flinn and Wirt (1965: 96–97); Hibbs (1977: 1470–1471).
56. Jennings (1979: 416); Merriam (1922: chapters 1, 13).
57. Cameron (1978); Castles (1982); Hibbs (1977); Jennings (1979); Nice (1985a); Tufte (1978: 92–104).
58. Nice and Cohen (1983); Plotnick and Winters (1985).
59. McGregor (1978); Munger and Blackhurst (1965).
60. Nice (1985a).
61. Savage (1978); Walker (1969).
62. Cowart (1969); Fleischmann and Nice (1988); Hofferbert and Urice (1985).
63. Walker (1971: 364).
64. March and Simon (1958: 184–185); Walker (1971: 369–370).
65. See Converse (1964); Ladd (1982: 33).
66. Nie, Verba, and Petrocik (1976: 112–115).
67. See Glendening and Reeves (1984: 44); Jennings and Zeigler (1970).
68. Zeigler and Tucker (1978: 256–260).
69. Edwards and Sharkansky (1978: 27–42); Verba and Nie (1972: chapter 3).
70. See Downs (1957: 136).
71. Eldersveld (1982: 56); Rose (1974: 4, chapter 15).
72. Rose (1974: 379).
73. Nie, Verba, and Petrocik (1976: 48–65).
74. Crotty and Jacobson (1980: 65–66); Sorauf (1980: 241–247).
75. For dissenting views of the party decline thesis, see Bibby, Cotter, Gibson, and Huckshorn (1983); Eldersveld (1982: 409–433).
76. Eyestone (1977: 441–443); Gray (1973: 1183–1185).
77. Savage (1978: 217).
78. See Sharkansky (1968: 47–48); Sundquist (1968: 498–505).

3

Teacher Competency Testing

Introduction

Education ranks as one of the most important responsibilities of state and local governments in the United States, partly because of the enormous expense and number of people involved. Education is the largest item in the typical state government budget and accounted for roughly 38 percent of all state spending in 1982. Moreover, approximately half of all state and local employment is in education. Public schools at the elementary and secondary levels enrolled over 35 million students per year during the early 1980s, and public colleges and universities served over 6 million students annually during the same period.[1] A program that involves huge amounts of money and enormous numbers of people is likely to attract substantial attention.

Education is also an important issue in state politics because of the many consequences of educational performance. If the schools cannot produce citizens prepared to assume their responsibilities in democratic government, the political system will suffer. If students do not acquire skills needed for employment and production, the economy will suffer. Businesses seeking to find suitably trained employees may decide to locate their operations elsewhere, so that the state tax base suffers. The failure to produce adequately trained personnel can also impair the nation's military capabilities.

In recent years, a growing chorus of critics has charged that the schools are not doing their job of educating students well. Student performance on standardized tests began a prolonged decline beginning in the mid-1960s. Research found that students in the United States performed poorly on achievement tests, at least when compared to students in other countries. The U.S. Navy found that roughly one fourth of its recruits could not read at the ninth-grade level, and 13 percent of all seventeen-year-olds are functionally illiterate. These signs of inadequate performance are particularly troubling because skill requirements and technological sophistication in many fields are rising each year. In the words of one influential study, "The educational foundations of our society are presently being eroded by a rising tide of mediocrity that threatens our future as a nation and a people."[2]

In addition to the comparatively systematic evidence on educational performance, individual cases add to concerns over the schools. Revelations of high school graduates who can barely read, write, or do simple arithmetic fuel additional complaints. Public confidence in the public schools has declined substantially from the early 1970s.[3] The chorus of complaints suggests a serious crisis.

Not all observers accept the premise of a crisis in the schools. Wirt argues that a longer time perspective, one that reaches back to the turn of the century, reveals considerable progress against illiteracy and progress in keeping young people in school.[4] In addition, much of the evidence used to document problems in the education system's performance is based on college admissions tests, which are not administered to all students. Much of the decline in SAT scores from 1963 through 1970 was apparently due to changes in the composition of the tested group, although the decline continued from 1970 through 1976 even though the composition of the group stabilized.[5] Even the most prominent critique of American schools admitted that the average American is better educated today than a generation ago.[6] In addition, public confidence in the public schools compares favorably with confidence in Congress, newspapers, big business, television, and organized labor.[7]

Close inspection of public evaluations of the schools also reveals an interesting pattern: People tend to regard the schools with which they are familiar more favorably (see Table 3.1). When respondents were asked to grade the public schools nationwide, only 27 percent of the respondents chose a grade of A or B. By contrast, when respondents were asked to grade the schools in their communities, 43 percent of all respondents (and 53 percent of all respondents with children in public schools) chose a grade of A or B. Respondents were even more positive in grading the public schools attended by their oldest child, fully 71 percent choosing A or B. Familiarity, in this case, breeds respect.[8]

Although the extent or existence of a crisis in the public schools remains controversial, many observers have expressed concerns regarding the system's performance. A number of studies in recent years have

TABLE 3.1. ■ Respondents' grading of the public schools

	Nationally	In their community		Attended by their oldest child
		all parents	public-school parents	
		(percent)		
A	3	9	8	23
B	24	34	44	48
C	43	30	33	19
D	12	10	9	5
E	3	4	4	2

SOURCE: *Gallup Report* (September 1985: 19–21). "Don't know" answers excluded.

explored the problem and have proposed a wide variety of solutions.[9] Dozens of state education commissions and task forces have produced hundreds of reform proposals of many types: more course requirements for high school graduation, increased instructional time, revision of teacher training programs, teacher performance incentives, and standardized examinations that students must pass to graduate have been discussed and adopted in numerous states. Although some observers have charged that many reforms have been adopted hastily and with too little analysis and reflection, the overall scope of reform activity is impressive.

Many of the education reforms are an outgrowth of charges that teachers are responsible for the performance of the schools. The critics complain that teachers are the less impressive college students and are often poorly qualified, especially in science and mathematics.[10] One of the proposed remedies is teacher competency testing: Anyone wishing to teach would be required to pass a test before being certified. As of 1983, twenty states had adopted competency testing for teachers,[11] and public support for competency testing is widespread.[12]

Although the subject-area coverage of teacher competency tests varies from state to state,[13] the basic premise is the same: Testing will weed out the less competent teachers[14] and stimulate others to perform at a higher level. Advocates of competency testing believe that these effects will in turn improve the educational performance of students. Whether these premises are correct and how large the improvements will be remain to be seen. Why some states have adopted teacher competency testing while others have not is the question to which I now turn.

Explaining Adoption

As noted earlier, a number of theories have been developed to explain adoption of innovations. The first holds that innovations result from experience with and orientations toward policy change. Officials and citizens in some states seem to take pride in being among the first to try new programs; people in some other states value caution and stability. In a similar vein, cultural norms that emphasize traditional values and practices may stifle change relative to cultural norms emphasizing progress, reform, and improvement. Moreover, if citizens and officials are accustomed to having policies that rarely change, proposals for doing anything new may meet with more resistance than where policy changes are common and therefore less shocking.

A second viewpoint holds that innovation results from the existence of organizational slack. Organizations that have more money, personnel, expertise, and other resources than they need to perform required functions can devote the surplus to developing and trying new programs and approaches. By contrast, organizations that must use all available resources to perform ongoing responsibilities will have little left to support innovations. Slack resources may be particularly important for policies like education; their immense costs may deter almost any policy change unless surplus resources are available. A new activity that adds a proportionally small amount to the education budget will still be adding many millions of dollars in costs, a prospect likely to deter change when resources are scarce.

A third perspective is that innovation results from a crisis or, less dramatically, from a perception that current programs and practices do not achieve the level of performance desired. What is considered an acceptable performance level is a function of many things, but one key element is often the performance levels of others.[15] If citizens believe that the services they receive are inferior to the services provided elsewhere, they may demand improvements. That pressure for improved performance may in turn produce innovations. According to this perspective, poor education performance is likely to spur adoption of competency testing to improve the performance of the schools.

A final, related possibility is that innovation is more likely when opposition to the innovation is relatively weak.[16] A well-organized, entrenched group of adversaries may derail changes even if other conditions are favorable. If those adversaries have many political resources at their disposal, they are more likely to be able to block adoption of innovations. Given that competency testing contains an implicit assumption that competency is deficient, educators might be expected to resent the implication and consequently the proposal on which it is based.

Analysis

The hypothesis that mandatory teacher competency testing is an outgrowth of a broader tendency toward innovativeness is strongly contradicted by the evidence (see Table 3.2). Less than one fourth of the most innovative states (innovation scores of .461 or higher) have adopted competency tests. By contrast, roughly two thirds of the least innovative states have adopted them. In short, the adopters tend to be states that are normally slow to do new things. Although a lack of experience with innovating on a regular basis may deter change in some cases, that pattern clearly does not hold for competency testing.

TABLE 3.2. ■ Competency tests and innovativeness

		Innovation score[a]			
		.406 or below	.407 to .460	.461 or higher	
Teacher competency test[b]	Yes	13 (68%)	3 (38%)	4 (22%)	
	No	6 (32%)	8 (62%)	14 (78%)	(gamma = −.63)
		100%	100%	100%	

[a]Walker (1971: 358). High scores indicate high degrees of innovativeness.
[b]Berland (1983: 13).

A related possibility is that adoption is facilitated by an ideological-cultural environment that favors or supports change. Where dominant norms place great emphasis on preserving established ways of doing things, advocates of change face a much more difficult task. According to Elazar, the "traditionalistic" political culture emphasizes preserving past practices and approaches and is suspicious of reform and social experimentation.[17] It should, therefore, stifle innovation.

This expectation is strongly contradicted by the data (see Table 3.3). Virtually all (94 percent) of the states with predominantly traditionalistic

TABLE 3.3. ■ Political culture and competency tests

		Political culture[a]		
		Other	Traditionalistic (T, TM, TI)	
Teacher competency test	Yes	5 (15%)	15 (94%)	
	No	29 (85%)	1 (6%)	(gamma = .98)
		100%	100%	

[a]Elazar (1972: 118).

political cultures have adopted mandatory competency testing, but relatively few of the other states have. While emphasis on tradition may stifle innovativeness in general, it clearly does not have that effect on this specific reform.[18]

Another aspect of the ideological environment is the state party system. If party ideologies emphasize preservation of traditional practices and values and discourage government activism, innovation may be less likely. Party ideologies emphasizing reform and government action, by contrast, may encourage innovation.

Once again, however, the evidence contradicts this perspective (see Table 3.4). States adopting competency testing tend to have conservative rather than liberal parties, particularly in the case of the Democratic party. More than four fifths of the states with the most conservative Democratic parties (McGregor scores of 4 or 5) have adopted competency testing, but less than one fifth of the states with more liberal Democratic parties have competency testing. In a similar fashion, over half the states with relatively conservative Republican parties (McGregor scores of 1 through 3) have adopted competency testing, but less than one fifth of the states with more liberal Republican parties have. Ideological liberalism may encourage reform and social experimentation generally, but clearly not in the case of competency testing.

TABLE 3.4. ■ Party ideology and teacher competency testing

		Democratic party ideology scores[a]			
		1–3		4–5	
Teacher competency	Yes	6	(19%)	14	(82%)	
testing	No	25	(81%)	3	(18%)	(gamma = .90)
			100%		100%	

		Republican party ideology scores[b]			
		1–3		4–5	
Teacher competency	Yes	17	(55%)	3	(18%)	
testing	No	14	(45%)	14	(82%)	(gamma = − .70)
			100%		100%	

[a]Low scores indicate liberalism.
[b]Low scores indicate conservatism.

The analysis to this point indicates that innovativeness in general and ideological receptivity to change cannot explain adoption of competency testing. A second possibility is that slack resources facilitate adoption. Creating the machinery needed to screen large numbers of prospective teachers and ensuring adequate security for the testing program could generate significant costs. Where surplus funds are scarce, those costs may discourage adoption of competency testing programs.

Once again, the evidence does not support this hypothesis (see Tables 3.5 and 3.6). Competency tests are most common in relatively poor states and in states with relatively low levels of expenditure per pupil. The parallel findings reflect the tendency for wealthier states to spend more money on education.[19] In a similar manner, competency testing is most common in states with relatively low teacher salaries, over half the states with below-average salaries adopting testing in contrast to fewer than one fourth of the states with average or above salaries. Slack resources, then, do not appear to yield adoption of competency testing.

TABLE 3.5. ■ Financial resources and teacher competency tests

		Median income, 1979[a]		
		Less than $19,400	Greater than $19,400	
Teacher competency test	Yes	14 (61%)	6 (22%)	
	No	9 (39%)	21 (78%)	(gamma = −.69)
		100%	100%	
		Education expenditure per pupil, 1980–81[b]		
		Below national mean	Above national mean	
Teacher competency test	Yes	16 (53%)	4 (20%)	
	No	14 (47%)	16 (80%)	(gamma = −.64)
		100%	100%	

[a]*Statistical Abstract* (1982: 437).
[b]*Book of the States* (1982: 442).

TABLE 3.6. ■ Teacher salaries and competency testing

		Teacher salaries, 1982[a]		
		Below national mean	Equal to/ above national mean	
Teacher competency test	Yes	16 (52%)	4 (21%)	
	No	15 (48%)	15 (79%)	(gamma = −.60)
		100%	100%	

[a]*Statistical Abstract* (1982: 152).

Having seen that we cannot explain the adoption of testing by a general tendency toward innovativeness, support for change and social reform, or slack resources, we now turn to a different approach, one that views innovations as a response to perceived inadequacy of system performance. When a system is not performing up to expectations, innovation may provide a plausible solution. Moreover, a system that is not performing adequately (or is so perceived) is likely to be more vulnerable to innovations imposed from outside.

Assessing the performance of the schools is a complicated process, partly because the schools try to perform many different tasks. Americans ask their schools to combat racial prejudice and segregation, eliminate illiteracy, foster good citizenship, provide entertainment, encourage upward mobility, train for jobs, increase appreciation of culture, and fight a wide variety of social problems from unsafe driving and venereal disease to hunger and inequality.[20] Almost any problem may become a responsibility of the schools.

Although the schools perform many functions, one of their most fundamental tasks is imparting basic skills, including literacy and a grasp of arithmetic. An educational system that produces a student who cannot read, write, or do simple arithmetic is unlikely to earn much respect, regardless of its achievements in other areas. If the schools do a relatively poor job of teaching those basic skills, citizens and officials may regard that situation as a crisis and demand educational innovations such as competency testing.

Analysis strongly supports this explanation (see Table 3.7). Competency tests are quite common in the states with the highest illiteracy rates and rare in the most literate states (illiteracy rates of 1 percent or less). In a similar fashion, three-fourths of the states that had 5.5 percent or more of their Selective Service inductees fail their mental examinations in 1973 (the last year for which there were inductees) have adopted competency tests, but only one seventh of the states with the lowest rejection rates has. Other evidence supports this position. The tests have been adopted throughout the South,[21] which has consistently ranked low on standardized national tests.[22] States whose educational systems have produced below-average final results, then, are the most likely to adopt mandatory competency testing.

TABLE 3.7. ■ Teacher competency test and education system performance

		Percentage illiterate, 1970[a]			
		1.0% or less	1.1% to 1.9%	2.0% or more	
Teacher compe-	Yes	2 (8%)	11 (65%)	7 (100%)	
tency test	No	24 (92%)	6 (35%)	0 (0%)	(gamma = .95)
		100%	100%	100%	

		Percentage of draftees failing mental tests, 1973[b]			
		2.5% or less	2.6% to 5.4%	5.5% or more	
Teacher compe-	Yes	3 (14%)	8 (47%)	9 (75%)	
tency test	No	18 (86%)	9 (53%)	3 (25%)	(gamma = .73)
		100%	100%	100%	

[a]Grant and Eiden (1982: 18).
[b]*Statistical Abstract* (1974: 323).

Innovations often generate opposition, and the strength of the opposition is a key factor in determining whether an innovation will be adopted. Competency testing, with its implication that some teachers are not competent, generated considerable opposition from the National Education Association (NEA), the largest teacher association in the country.[23] However, the NEA has recently come to accept competency testing, if somewhat reservedly. To the extent that educators have opposed competency testing, states where teachers are in a better position to block adoption of testing should be less likely to adopt it.

One important aspect of the ability of educators to block competency programs is the legal environment for teacher participation in educational decision making. A legal environment supportive of teacher influence (and perhaps reflecting teacher influence) should therefore reduce the prospects of adopting competency testing. Perhaps one of the most notable legal provisions affecting teacher influence is the recognition of educators' right to bargain collectively. Although the behavior of teacher organizations does not always conform to official policies, the presence of supportive laws reduces the likelihood of teachers being ignored and may reflect a recognition of their role in decision making.

Analysis reveals that states with mandatory collective bargaining laws covering primary and secondary professional education personnel are relatively unlikely to have adopted competency tests but that most of the states without collective bargaining laws have adopted competency testing (see Table 3.8). The clearest tendency obtains for states with collective bargaining provisions that include the right to strike: not one has adopted competency testing. The findings presented in Table 3.7 are also pertinent to the question of educator opposition, for where the schools appear to be doing a poor job, educators will be in a relatively weak position to oppose policy changes.[24]

Multivariate analysis of the influences on the adoption of competency testing indicates that system performance and political culture ap-

TABLE 3.8. ■ Competency tests and collective bargaining policies in education

		State had mandatory collective bargaining law for primary and secondary professional education personnel[a]		
		Yes		
		Strikes permitted	No strikes permitted	No
Teacher competency test	Yes	0 (0%)	6 (29%)	14 (64%)
	No	7 (100%)	15 (71%)	8 (36%) (gamma = .76)
		100%	100%	100%

[a]*Book of the States* (1982: 443). Laws providing only for meeting and conferring coded as not providing mandatory collective bargaining.

pear to be the key factors in shaping state decisions (see Table 3.9).[25] States adopting testing are those with relatively high illiteracy rates and traditionalistic political cultures. The latter tendency is not consistent with the expected relationship between culture and innovation but is consistent with the traditionalistic culture's emphasis on hierarchical control.[26] Clearly, competency testing has been imposed on educators from outside, notably by governors and legislators. The traditionalistic culture, by emphasizing control from the top down, evidently encourages governors and legislators to adopt competency testing in spite of educator opposition. In addition, higher illiteracy rates indicate poorer system performance—a crisis of sorts that evidently stimulates an innovative response.

TABLE 3.9. ■ Discriminant analysis of adoption of state teacher competency testing

	All states	Alaska and Hawaii omitted
Canonical correlation	.77	.78
Wilks's lambda	.41	.40
Chi²	41.63[a]	41.31[a]
Cases correctly classified	88%	86%[b]
Group centroids[c]		
Group 0	−.95	−1.01
Group 1	1.43	1.42
Standardized canonical		
Discriminant function coefficients		
% illiterate	.36	.54
Traditionalism	.75	.56

[a]Significant at the .0001 level with 2 degrees of freedom.
[b]Prediction is for all 50 states based on coefficients derived from the continental 48.
[c]Group 0 = no competency testing; Group 1 = competency testing.

The canonical correlation, which indicates the degree of association between the discriminant function and adoption of competency testing (equivalent to a multiple correlation coefficient when the dependent variable is a dichotomy, as here) is quite high, as is the percentage of cases correctly classified—that is, behaving as predicted by the model.[27] In a similar manner, Wilk's lambda, which is low when the model is relatively successful in discriminating among the groups defined by the dependent variable, is respectably low. The group centroids are relatively far from one another, which again indicates that the model is generally able to distinguish between states that have adopted competency testing and those that have not.

The standardized canonical discriminant function coefficients, which are analogous to beta weights in regression analysis, reveal that higher illiteracy rates and traditionalistic political cultures are positively associated with adoption of competency testing. The relative importance of illiteracy and culture, however, is relatively sensitive to which cases are included in the analysis. With all fifty states included, political culture is considerably more important than illiteracy. When Alaska and Hawaii are omitted, the two predictors are about equally influential. The shift occurs because both states have above-average illiteracy rates but not competency testing and are therefore outliers.

Overall, the evidence supports the view that competency testing is an innovation that emerged in an environment of poor organizational performance and a political culture that emphasizes hierarchical control. Hypotheses that competency tests reflect innovativeness in general, cultural factors supporting change, or slack resources are strongly contradicted by the data.

Discussion and Conclusions

Members of a profession often complain that they do not recruit enough of the brightest and best people, a situation that stems in part from the tendency for expectations to outrun available supplies.[28] Many critics of American education have charged that the education profession has failed to recruit the best talent.[29] Competency testing has been advanced as a partial solution to that problem.

The adoption of this reform is heavily concentrated in states that are generally slow to adopt new programs and have cultures emphasizing tradition, not change and reform. Moreover, the adopters are generally states that have few slack resources, as measured by state wealth and by education spending per pupil. This particular reform seems to flow in large measure from inadequate organizational performance and a culture emphasizing elite control.

Why, however, should the innovation appear now? State rankings in illiteracy rates have been relatively stable for several decades, and the same can be said for teacher salaries.[30] Relative performance gaps are not new. Two factors may account for the timing of this innovation.

First, declining student performance on standardized national tests[31] has led to massive publicity and attention devoted to the issue of educational performance. Undoubtedly, that attention generated particular discomfort where performance was even worse than the declining average. A relatively poor performance that attracts little attention is less likely to stimulate reform efforts.

Second, the rapid economic growth in the South in recent years,[32] with concomitant industrialization and commercialization, has created new demands for skilled employees. The performance of the schools has therefore received added attention, a situation reflected in the fact that the first seven states to adopt competency testing were all located in the South. An educational system that is reasonably adequate for a rural-oriented agricultural society may be less suitable in an urbanized industrial-commercial economy.

If pressures for change are present, what accounts for the appeal of competency testing? It is by no means the only education reform adopted in recent years,[33] but it is one of the most widely adopted. On close inspection, its appeal is not surprising in light of alternative strategies.

A number of other education reforms have a common shortcoming: high cost. Because teacher salaries make up a large majority of total education costs, substantial increases in teacher salaries are extremely expensive. In addition, salary increases may be of limited value unless they are directed to better teachers and to specialties in short supply.[34] The combination of high costs and administrative complications is discouraging, particularly in light of continuing opposition to education tax increases in many circles.[35] Longer school years and school days also bring the prospect of major cost increases.

Other approaches present major implementation problems. If declining family stability contributes to discipline problems, how can family stability be increased? If families do not encourage and reward learning, how can that be changed? If student learning is impaired by drug and alcohol abuse, do policymakers have a dependable remedy? If student devotion to study is limited by the many distractions of modern life, can that be changed? Workable solutions seem to be in short supply.

In this context, teacher competency testing has great appeal. It makes essentially no demands on the average citizen and is comparatively inexpensive to the taxpayer, especially if a fee is charged for taking the test. Administering tests is not particularly difficult, especially in contrast to increasing family stability or convincing people not to consume mind-altering substances. Competency testing, then, emerges as a comparatively easy innovation. As a solution, however, it has a basic limitation.

Given the strong tendency for states with competency testing to have below-average teacher salaries, it is not clear how testing can improve teacher quality without efforts to make teaching more rewarding at the same time. Beyond some point, higher standards without higher compensation may create shortages of qualified personnel, particularly in specialties that can earn higher salaries in business and industry. If the state's economy has difficulty supporting higher salaries, however, state officials may have little choice but to go with testing, making such efforts to enhance the attractiveness of teaching as circumstances permit.

Finally, in a time when cynicism about government is rampant, the findings of this analysis indicate that governments can and do respond to evidence of inadequate performance. This is not to say that advocates of innovations can always expect an enthusiastic reception for their proposals or that the responses will be successful. The pattern of adoptions of competency testing does indicate the existence of feedback in the policy-making process and efforts to improve system outputs.

NOTES

See Bibliography for full reference.

1. *Book of the States* (1984: 274, 322, 363).
2. *A Nation at Risk* (1983: 5; see also pp. 8–10); Wirt (1983: 317).
3. *Gallup Report* (1985a: 3).
4. Wirt (1983: 317–320).
5. Rosenblatt (1985: 68–69).
6. *Nation at Risk* (1983: 11).
7. *Gallup Report* (1985a: 3).
8. For similar findings regarding bureaucracies in general, see Katz, Gutek, Kahn, and Barton (1975: 120–124).
9. See *Nation at Risk* (1983); *Book of the States* (1984: 353–356); Dye (1988: 414–415); Wirt and Gove (1990: 465–466).
10. *Nation at Risk* (1983: 22–23); Thompson (1985a: 55–57).
11. Berland (1983).
12. *Gallup Report* (1985b: 22).
13. Berland (1983: 13).
14. The tests adopted as of 1983 were limited to teachers who were not certified.
15. March and Simon (1958: 183).
16. Mohr (1969: 111, 114).
17. Elazar (1972: 99–102).
18. States with predominantly traditionalistic political cultures clearly tend to be less innovative generally, as measured by Walker (1971: 358). Roughly two thirds (21 of 32) of the states that are not predominantly traditionalistic have innovation scores above the national median, but less than one fifth of the predominantly traditionalistic states score above the national median.
19. Dye (1988: 419).
20. Dye (1988: 410–411); Wirt (1983: 303–304).
21. Berland (1983: 13).
22. Grant and Eiden (1982: 25–32); Wirt (1983: 317).
23. Berland (1983: 13).
24. Pupil performance is a function of many factors, only some under the educational system's control.
25. All of the independent variables from Tables 3.2–3.8 except party ideology were included in the multivariate analysis. Party ideology was excluded because the direction of the relationships contradicted the hypothesis. Variables that had no independent predictive

power were then removed from the analysis, and the model was reestimated to produce the findings in Table 3.9.

26. Elazar (1972: 99–101); Wirt (1983: 308).
27. For an introduction to discriminant analysis, see Klecka (1980).
28. See Merton (1965: 53–56).
29. Berland (1983); Thompson (1985a: 55–57).
30. Wirt (1983: 321).
31. Wirt (1983: 317).
32. See Break (1980: 26–27).
33. See *The Nation Responds* (1984).
34. Chance (1986: 138–145).
35. Thompson (1985b: 4).

Balanced Budget Amendment to the U.S. Constitution

Introduction

One of the fascinating aspects of policy innovation in the United States is the ability of one level of government in the federal system to foster policy innovation by another level. The national government has used grants-in-aid to stimulate state and local innovation.[1] The adoption of the 55 MPH speed limit, for example, was spurred by a requirement attached to national highway aid. U.S. Supreme Court decisions have, with varying degrees of effectiveness, brought about state and local reforms ranging from school desegregation to advising criminal suspects of their constitutional rights. The states have used their considerable legal and financial powers over local governments to foster all sorts of local policy innovations, ranging from local government reorganization to provision of services.

In a similar fashion, lower levels of government often encourage innovation by higher levels. Local government officials have lobbied state and national governments to create new financial aid programs. Programs adopted at the state level have later been adopted by the national government, in part because the track record of programs in use helps to reduce the uncertainty that otherwise discourages innovation. Officials who serve in one level of government and then move up to a higher level may carry practices used at one level to another level.

In recent years, a number of groups seeking the adoption of new national policies have pursued the strategy of using the states to foster adoption of national policy changes. The U.S. Constitution provides that a constitutional convention shall be called by Congress "on the application of the legislatures of two-thirds" of the states and that proposed amendments may be ratified by the legislatures of three fourths of the states.[2] One group pursuing that strategy is concerned with national budget deficits.

Budget deficits have been a chronic feature of the national political landscape for the past two decades. Those recurrent deficits have led to calls for a constitutional amendment requiring a balanced federal budget.[3] Proponents of the amendment contend that pressures to increase spending have overwhelmed the national government's ability to raise revenue, a situation that results in persistent deficits.[4] The triumph of Keynesian economic theory, with its call for deficits when the economy needs stimulation, led to a greater acceptance of deficits under all circumstances.[5] In the era prior to the Great Depression, deficits were generally regarded as unacceptable, regardless of the performance of the economy. Deficits did occur, however; between 1894 and 1914, the national government had budget deficits for eleven years.[6] Officials generally felt an obligation to try to balance the budget, occasional lapses notwithstanding. When deficits gained respectability as a method of fighting recessions, the risk of deficits during periods of prosperity increased.

According to the restraining rules and process model,[7] normal political processess are not likely to correct the situation. Organized interest groups and government bureaucrats press for expansion of programs, many of which have substantial public support. Elected officials, generally anxious to retain their jobs, provide increased funding for those programs, but taxpayers resist increases in revenues, a situation that yields persistent deficits. The only solution, in this view, lies in the adoption of strict regulations such as a constitutional amendment requiring a balanced federal budget.

The restraining rules and process model gained additional credibility when the national government's budget deficits ballooned following the election of President Ronald Reagan, a conservative who repeatedly emphasized his desire to balance the federal budget. While much of the deficit during the Reagan years reflected the performance of the economy,[8] the president's inability to translate his desire for a balanced budget into results underscored the difficulties inherent in reducing the deficits.

Enter the States

As concern over the national deficits grew, a number of states, beginning in 1975, enacted legislative resolutions calling for a national constitutional convention to propose an amendment requiring a balanced federal budget. Many states have imposed similar requirements on themselves for years. Advocates of the national requirement have often emphasized the long experience states have had with balanced budget requirements. However, relatively little attention has been paid to evidence on the effectiveness of the state requirements. A brief overview of the record at the state level may provide clues to what would result from a national balanced budget amendment.[9]

The evidence indicates that for a number of reasons constitutional balanced budget requirements and debt limits are not particularly effective in controlling state deficits and debt. First, state limitations on deficits generally apply only to the operating budget and exclude the capital budget.[10] (The capital budget includes purchases of relatively durable items, such as building and heavy equipment, which are expected to produce benefits for a number of years.) As a result of the separate operating and capital budgets, a state may simultaneously balance the former and run a large deficit in the latter.

Limitations on deficits and indebtedness at the state level are also circumvented by the use of nonguaranteed debt and special authorities. Nonguaranteed debt does not have a legal claim on the state treasury but is paid off only by the proceeds of a specific project such as a toll bridge. Because nonguaranteed debt makes no claim on the general treasury, debt limits generally do not apply. Special authorities, such as state-chartered instrumentalities, may be given authority to issue bonds of their own. These bonds, which have no claim on the state treasury but only on the proceeds of the special authority, are generally not affected by state budget requirements or debt limits.[11] One indication of the use of these devices is the fact that 64 percent of all state long-term debt was nonguaranteed in 1982.[12]

A balanced budget requirement may encourage even greater use of authorities that are not officially part of the budget and whose borrowing is not counted in assessing the size of the deficit.[13] The budget would tell less and less about what government programs were doing. Balanced budget requirements may stimulate the use of off-budget items, such as guaranteed loans, rather than expenditures,[14] with the result that the fiscal effects of government grow harder to assess and less amenable to control and oversight through the budget process. State debt restrictions may also encourage shifting of indebtedness to local units,[15] so that total indebtedness is unaffected by the restriction.

Finally, balanced budget requirements may encourage an administration to choose policies that are less expensive now but more expensive in the future, a problem that will presumably trouble a later administration.[16]

We should not be surprised to learn that research indicates little relationship between debt limitations and actual state-local debt.[17] In addition, only half of the states' chief budget officers cite debt restrictions (which 37 states have) as important in prohibiting deficit spending.[18] Balanced budget requirements also require accurate forecasts of revenues and expenditures; in turn, that requires accurate forecasts of the performance of the economy. In recent years, experts have often produced widely varying projections of economic conditions, revenues, and expenditures. Knowing whose projections to use raises a difficult problem. In addition, inaccurate projections may force traumatic midyear budgetary revisions to compensate for revenue shortfalls or unexpectedly high spending. Officials may be tempted to manipulate forecasts to comply technically with the balanced budget requirement. That manipulation occurs to some degree in any case, but it is much more attractive when the forecasts are directly linked to revenue and spending decisions.[19]

If a balanced budget requirement forces midyear budget revisions, they might exaggerate economic fluctuations as well, at least during recessions. They typically cause declines in revenues and cost increases, at least for some programs (such as unemployment compensation). Cutting spending or raising additional revenues during a recession can make the recession even worse. That problem can be reduced by budgets that are projected to have a modest surplus; in that case, a modest revenue shortfall will produce a smaller surplus or a balanced budget instead of a deficit. Bear in mind that if budget surpluses had enough political support to gain adoption, no one would be interested in a balanced budget requirement. Moreover, persistent national budget surpluses would risk slowing the economy and causing a recession.[20]

Despite the mixed record of balanced budget requirements and debt limits at the state level, a number of states have them, and a number support a similar requirement nationally. Why have some states called for a national balanced budget amendment while others have not?

Potential Influences

As noted in Chapter 2, whether an innovation attracts support may depend on its compatibility with the broader environment. A potentially significant aspect of that environment is whether a state itself is bound by a balanced budget requirement or a constitutional debt limit. However, the nature of the relationship is difficult to predict.

At first glance we might suspect that belief in balanced budgets would produce consistent state orientations, with states that support a national balanced budget amendment imposing similar constitutional requirements on themselves. In this view, orientations toward specific innovation—a balanced budget requirement—should produce consistency. But an alternative possibility must be considered. Fiscal limitations placed on one level of government may serve to broaden the fiscal options of another level.[21] In this view, states might support a national balanced budget requirement in part to give themselves readier access to borrowed funds—a form of problem or crisis innovation. Historically, state and local borrowing has generally been heaviest when national borrowing has been lightest.[22] To the degree that balanced budget requirements reflect preferences regarding which level should have more financial power or broader options, then, support for the requirement at one level may not ensure support for the same requirements applied to other levels.

Another potential source of differences between support for national balanced budget requirements on one hand and support for state requirements on the other stems from the operation of fiscal federalism. If subnational governments try to use budget deficits or surpluses to alter the performance of the economy, much of the effect is diluted by leakages to other jurisdictions. Only the national government can have much impact on the economy through fiscal policy.[23] State officials, then, might properly regard state and national balanced budget requirements differently.

Analysis of the consistency of state support for the constitutional balanced budget requirements at the national and state levels must consider two types of state provisions. The first requires that the budget or legislative appropriations must be balanced. The second places a limitation on the amount of state debt. The two provisions are often found together and cannot be considered alternative means to the same end. The decision to place these provisions in the state constitution represents a higher degree of commitment to balanced budgets and debt restrictions than writing them into ordinary law, for constitutional provisions are much more difficult to change.[24]

Ideological factors may also influence state support for balanced budget requirements. In general, conservatives oppose government activism and government intervention in the economy. Liberals are more willing to use government power to attack social problems, including the use of fiscal policy to manage the economy.[25] Liberals fear that a balanced budget requirement would deprive the federal government of a major tool for stimulating the economy.[26] In a serious recession, deficit spending would be unavailable for stimulating the economy or would require an extraordinary legislative majority. The result could be a recession longer and more severe than would have been the case if deficit spending had been possible.[27] Conservatives, by contrast, believe the balanced budget requirement will promote fiscal discipline. Only if policymakers must combine the joy of spending with the pain of raising taxes will they give spending programs the close scrutiny needed to avoid wasteful expenditures.[28] In addition, monetary policy would remain to manage the economy if a balanced budget amendment became law.[29] Conservatives might support the balanced budget amendment as a reaction to the problem of chronic deficits.

Four ideology measures will be used in this analysis. Two measures of the ideologies of state Democratic and Republican parties were developed by McGregor.[30] To the degree that many citizens are relatively uninterested in budgetary issues, party ideologies may play a crucial role in shaping state decisions. Organized support for conservative or liberal beliefs may make the difference between passage and defeat.

The other measures seek to capture the ideological leanings of state electorates. The percentage of the two-party vote going to George McGovern in the 1972 presidential election, which was strongly influenced by ideological and issue factors and relatively weakly influenced by party loyalties, indicates how citizens respond to concrete political choices. In addition, estimates of state opinion based on surveys tell us how citizens view themselves.[31] To the degree that public officials respond to public desires, states with more conservative electorates should be more likely to call for a balanced budget amendment.

Support for a balanced budget may also be affected by the competiveness of the state party system. With party competition, and the uncertainty it brings, politicians have a greater incentive to keep their options open because of the need to bid for votes. In the competitive context, votes are valuable, so the question of what will please voters in an upcoming election is always salient.[32] Amending a constitution may foreclose an option that may later be politically appealing. Officials in politically competitive states should therefore be less likely to support calls for a national amendment. To the degree that those state officials hope to move on to national office, they are likely to be reluctant to support an amendment that will force national officials to make painful choices.

Party competition will be measured by indexes based on legislative and gubernatorial elections and results.[33] Both indexes give high scores to states in which both parties elect a large proportion of the state legislature and each party controls the governor's mansion on a regular basis. Conversely, states with low scores have one party controlling the vast majority of legislative seats and the governor's mansion all or most of the time. The Ranney index covers 1962–1973, and the Bibby index covers 1974–1980. The latter is more contemporary in coverage but seems to be distorted somewhat by the pro-Democratic surge after Watergate.

The budgetary environment may also influence state orientations toward balanced budget requirements. Officials in states that are relatively successful in attracting federal resources may feel little inclination to restrain federal fiscal powers and may be more wary of alienating federal officials. States that are more successful in attracting federal revenues have more to lose and may be more reluctant to support changes that threaten that beneficial relationship. Success in attracting federal funds, then, may stimulate opposition to a balanced budget amendment or fears that such an amendment would yield cuts in federal aid and therefore create financial problems.

The relative positions of states receiving federal largesse can be measured in a number of ways. Perhaps the simplest is federal grants per capita, which indicates the financial resources each person in the state would have to replace if federal aid was lost. A slightly more complex measure is federal grants as a percentage of total state and local general revenue. The use of this measure is based on the premise that a loss of 25 percent of total revenues would produce more painful program cuts than a loss of 10 percent of total revenue. The most inclusive measure of national-state fiscal relations is total federal expenditures in a state divided by total federal revenues derived from a state.[34] This measure includes nongrant expenditures, which are substantial, and considers what a state has contributed to federal revenues as well as what is received.

One other fiscal element that may influence state support for balanced budget requirements is affluence. Officials in a wealthy state may feel more confident of their ability to function well without federal aid or with substantial aid reductions that might follow a balanced budget amendment. They would therefore feel freer to support a national requirement—a variant of the slack-innovation hypothesis. At the same time, wealthier people tend to be conservative on economic matters,[35] which should further enhance support for the national requirement in wealthier states.

Other elements of the socioeconomic environment that may influence state responses to the balanced budget issue are urbanization and education. As noted earlier, rural and small-town areas lack some of the social problems of larger cities and lack contact with people from areas where those social problems exist. Consequently, rural and small-town residents are reluctant to give government power and authority to deal with those problems. Urbanization, with its greater social interdependence, creates a need for some institution to cope with the demands and problems of an urban society. The antigovernment views of rural and small-town residents, more common in rural states, may make those states more supportive of a balanced budget requirement.

The influence of education on balanced budget requirements is difficult to assess in its direct effects, but an indirect effect can be predicted. As a general rule, educated people are more likely to think about politics in ideological ways and to display consistency in their policy attitudes.[36] They may therefore be more inclined to make the connection between program benefits and revenue considerations that the balanced budget requires. Higher levels of education, by promoting ideological, consistent thinking, may produce greater support for balanced budget requirements.[37]

State support for the national requirement is measured by the passage of a state legislative resolution calling for a national amendment.[38] Although failure to pass such a resolution does not necessarily mean opposition to a balanced federal budget in principle, it does indicate an unwillingness to advocate a constitutional amendment and therefore less support for a balanced federal budget than displayed by states that have called for a convention.

Analysis

The findings presented in Table 4.1 clearly indicate that state support for a federal constitutional balanced budget does not spring from the same sources as similar requirements in state constitutions. Whether a state's legislature has passed a resolution calling for the national constitutional requirement is unrelated to whether the state constitution requires a balanced budget or limits debt (r's of $-.03$ and $.13$, respectively).[39]

The zero-order relationships do support the hypothesis that ideolog-

TABLE 4.1. ■ Zero-order relationships in state support for a constitutional balanced budget requirement and state characteristics

	Call for national balanced budget
Balanced budget for state[a]	− .03
Fixed debt limit for state[b]	.13
Republican ideology[c]	− .30[f]
Democratic ideology[d]	.34[g]
McGovern vote, 1972	− .60[h]
Electoral conservatism[e]	.51[h]
Party competition	
1974–1980	− .08
1962–1973	− .36[h]
Median income	− .24[f]
Percent metro	− .23
Percent high school graduates	− .05
Federal grants as a percentage of S-L revenue	− .08
Federal spending divided by federal revenue	.28[f]
Federal grants per capita	− .10

[a]State constitution requires balanced budget and/or balanced appropriations.
[b]Deficits prohibited or subject to limitation by state constitution.
[c]Low values indicate conservatism.
[d]Low values indicate liberalism.
[e]Value for Nevada is adjusted; see Wright, Erikson, and McIver (1985: 478–480).
[f]Significant at the .05 level; correlations are Pearson's r's.
[g]Significant at the .01 level.
[h]Significant at the .005 level.

ical forces shape state responses to national budget issues. States calling for a balanced national budget have more conservative Republican and Democratic parties and more conservative electorates. The relationships for measures of electoral ideology are particularly strong; indeed, they are the strongest of any in Table 4.1.

As expected, states with more competitive political parties in 1962–1973 are less likely to call for an amendment. The same pattern does not appear when competition is measured from 1974 through 1980, perhaps because of the distortions of the post-Watergate surge noted earlier.

Socioeconomic characteristics present a mixed pattern in accounting for state decisions on the balanced budget issue. Contrary to the slack innovation hypothesis, wealthier states are less likely to call for a national amendment than poorer states. More metropolitan states are somewhat less likely to call for a balanced budget, but education levels are virtually unrelated to state decisions.

The operation of fiscal federalism produces similarly mixed results. States that receive large amounts of federal spending relative to the federal revenues they contribute are particularly likely to call for an amendment, a finding that may contain a valuable lesson for students of gratitude. The other measures of federal aid, however, are essentially unrelated to state decisions on this issue.

The absence of any substantial relationships between state constitutional budget requirements and debt limits on one hand and state calls for a national requirement on the other casts considerable doubt on the argument that the calls grow from a consistent viewpoint on balanced budgets in general, a desire to make both levels play by the same fiscal rules, or an inclination to broaden the financial options of one level by restricting the options of another.

By contrast, all the ideological variables perform as hypothesized, greater conservatism being associated with states calling for the national amendment. That pattern can be interpreted as a type of crisis innovation to the degree that conservatives are particularly concerned about the deficit problem. In addition, however, the impact of ideology could reflect the importance of views regarding governmental responsibilities and opposition to an innovation, with liberals being particularly anxious to preserve national fiscal options.

The zero-order findings offer little support for the slack-resources model. Wealthier states are less likely to call for a national requirement, and federal aid success as an indicator of resource availability is virtually unrelated to state calls for a national requirement. The somewhat broader federal-spending-relative-to-federal-revenue variable is consistent with the slack-innovation model, but viewed in the context of other indicators of slack resources, that finding seems less than compelling.

Discriminant analysis of whether each state has passed a resolution calling for the amendment produces a two-variable model (see Table 4.2). States that have called for the amendment tend to have more conservative electorates, with both measures emerging in the model. The McGovern vote is a somewhat stronger predictor than the survey-based

TABLE 4.2. ■ Discriminant analysis of state calls for a constitutional requirement for a balanced federal budget

		Standardized canonical discriminant function coefficents	
Percent for McGovern, 1972		.75	
Electoral conservatism		−.53	
Canonical correlation	.66	*Group centroids*[a]	
Wilks's lambda	.56	Group 0	1.18
Chi²	26.206[b]	Group 1	−.64
Percent of cases correctly classified	83.33		

[a]Group 0: State has not called for a federal balanced budget amendment. Group 1: State has called for a federal balanced budget amendment. Alaska and Hawaii omitted because of missing data.
[b]Significant at the .0001 level with two degrees of freedom.

measure of opinion, but both variables make significant contributions. Public sentiments emerge as the decisive factor.

The discriminant analysis is quite successful in accounting for state decisions on the issue. The analysis correctly predicts the behavior of 83 percent of the states. None of the other variables in Table 4.1 provides noticeable added predictive power.

The multivariate analysis is consistent with the view that the drive for the national amendment draws disproportionate support from politically conservative states. However, there is no relationship between whether a state has called for a national balanced budget amendment and whether the state has a balanced budget requirement or debt limit in its own constitution, once ideological factors are taken into account. Moreover, slack resources are also unrelated to state responses to the national issue when ideological factors are controlled.

The inability of slack resources to account for state calls is hardly surprising. In an immediate sense, a state incurs no significant costs in passing a resolution calling for a national amendment. Of course, a national requirement, should it prove effective (bear in mind that the state record suggests otherwise), might very well trigger cuts in federal aid to the states. A number of members of Congress proposed doing precisely that as more states passed balanced budget resolutions.[40] Relatively speaking, however, the costs of adopting new state-tax relief programs or opening a major university are likely to be immediate and tangible. The costs that a state might incur by calling for a national balanced budget are distant and uncertain. The availability of slack resources in that context may make little difference.

Conclusions

Analysis of state responses to constitutional budget requirements reveals that state support depends upon the target of the requirement. There is virtually no relationship beween state calls for a national constitutional requirement and the existence of such state constitutional requirements. State responses to the national budget issue appear to flow largely from ideological influences. States with conservative electorates are particularly likely to support the national amendment, a position consistent with conservatives' mistrust of national governmental power and efforts to regulate the functioning of the economy as well as their belief in the need for fiscal discipline.

The pattern of state responses to the national amendment is consistent with Schattschneider's concept of the "scope of conflict," which holds that the magnitude of a conflict often determines which side wins.[41] As a result, individuals and groups will seek to decrease, maintain, or increase the scope of conflict to produce the level most likely to yield the outcome they desire. Interjurisdictional competition among states for jobs, investment, and wealth makes them more vulnerable than the national government to pressure from upper-status interests.[42] It is therefore not surprising to find that relatively conservative states are particularly likely to support the drive to limit national fiscal powers through the amendment. The result would be to lower the scope of conflict on some fiscal matters to the state level where the prospects for conservative success are greater.

Bear in mind that calling for a national amendment may have no impact if too few states pass similar resolutions or the proposed amendment is not ratified. In that case, the resolution is a symbolic act, an affirmation of a valued principle. To the degree that state officials regard a legislative resolution calling for a balanced budget amendment as a relatively costless way to express their beliefs or the beliefs of their constituents, ideological forces are free to exert influence without the constraints of resource considerations.

NOTES

See Bibliography for full reference.

1. Walker (1969: 895); Welch and Thompson (1980).
2. Amendments may be proposed by a two-thirds majority of both houses of Congress and may be ratified by conventions in three fourths of the states (see Pritchett, 1977: 26–29).
3. Wright (1982: 240–241).
4. See Break (1980: 256–260).
5. See Buchanan and Flowers (1987; 133, 146).
6. Wildavsky (1988: 52).
7. Break 1980: 256–260).
8. On the relationship between the economy and budget deficits, see Lowery (1985).
9. State experiences with debt limitations and balanced budget requirements may not necessarily translate to the national level in all respects. Capital budgets, which are common at the state level, are not used at the national level. Differences in administrative expertise and legislative oversight could produce different results. Nonetheless, some possible lessons may be learned from the states' experiences.
10. *Limitations on State Deficits* (1976: 3).
11. Maxwell and Aronson (1977: 209–214).
12. *Book of the States* (1984: 326).
13. Rosen (1985: 233).
14. Break (1980: 259–260). The guaranteed loan device involves the government guaranteeing that private lenders who loan money to support a particular activity will be compensated for any losses they incur. The true cost of the loan guarantee is not known

until some future date when lenders encounter problems with borrowers who cannot or will not repay the loans.

15. Break (1980: 259–260).
16. Wildavsky (1974: 73).
17. Maxwell and Aronson (1977: 207).
18. *Limitations on State Deficits* (1976: 7).
19. Buchanan and Flowers (1987: 171); Rosen (1985: 233).
20. Buchanan and Flowers (1987: 171); Musgrave and Musgrave (1980: 15); Sharp and Olson (1978: 324–326).
21. Break (1980: 259–260).
22. Maxwell and Aronson (1977: 189).
23. Musgrave and Musgrave (1980: 526–527).
24. Lockard (1963: 89–90).
25. Dolbeare and Dolbeare (1976: 56–69, 73–77); Sargent (1981: 65–70).
26. Shannon and Wallin (1979).
27. Aronson (1985: 264–265).
28. See Musgrave and Musgrave (1980: 621); Shannon and Wallin (1979).
29. Aronson (1985: 264).
30. McGregor (1978).
31. Wright, Erikson, and McIver (1985).
32. Downs (1957: 111); Schattschneider (1960: 80).
33. Ranney (1976); Bibby, Cotter, Gibson, and Huckshorn (1983).
34. Hanson (1983: 50).
35. Erikson, Luttbeg, and Tedin (1980: 154–155).
36. Asher (1980: 119–120); Nie, Verba, and Petrocik (1976: 120–121, 148–150).
37. As noted earlier, not all ideologies support balanced budgets, but without some degree of ideological or consistent thinking, individuals may be more prone simultaneously to prefer lower taxes and higher spending. On the existence of that tendency among less-educated people, see Axelrod (1967).
38. National Taxpayers Union (1984). States not adopting resolutions include California, Connecticut, Hawaii, Illinois, Kentucky, Maine, Massachusetts, Michigan, Minnesota, Montana, New Jersey, New York, Ohio, Rhode Island, Vermont, Washington, West Virginia, and Wisconsin.
39. Constitutional balanced budget requirements are found in 24 states; 37 have constitutional debt limits, and 14 have both (*Book of the States,* 1982: 368).
40. Wright (1982: 240–241).
41. Schattschneider (1960).
42. See Nice (1987c).

5

Sunset Laws

Introduction

America's state legislatures have a wide variety of responsibilities, including enacting laws, resolving political conflicts, proposing state constitutional amendments, confirming executive appointments, handling impeachments, enacting budgets, and overseeing the operation of the state bureaucracy.[1] Overseeing the bureaucracy is a crucial legislative task, but it also presents legislators with a painful dilemma.

Vigorous legislative oversight offers numerous benefits to state legislatures and the state as a whole. Legislators may learn a great deal about social problems and program operations through active oversight. Regular oversight can reduce the risk that agencies will misinterpret or ignore legislative directives. Administrators may put forth more effort if they expect periodic legislative assessments of their productivity. Consistent oversight may help to prevent corruption in agency operations.

However, oversight also presents legislators with a number of potential problems. Legislators may be hesitant to confront state administrators who possess greater training and expertise in their fields. Oversight may irritate the governor, who may regard it as meddling or intrusion in executive affairs. People who benefit from agency programs may not welcome legislative efforts to check on agency operations.

Legislative oversight has been hampered by the many other demands on legislative time and energy. By the time members finish with a large volume of legislation, confirm a number of executive appointees, and complete action on the state budget, little time or inclination for oversight may remain. Finally, oversight is often believed to have limited political payoff; in the absence of a spectacular scandal or disaster, oversight may not be as impressive to the voters as a new state program or a series of impressive speeches.[2] As a result, oversight has often received less attention than it deserves.[3]

Legislative oversight of the bureaucracy can be conducted in many ways.[4] In considering agency budget requests, legislators may examine agency performance and determine whether legislative intentions have been followed in the implementation of programs. Budget hearings also give legislators an opportunity to inform agency officials of legislative desires, formally and informally. The prospect of continued funding is a dependable way to gain the attention of administrators. However, the complexity of agency budgets and the pressure of time may mean that budget hearings are too perfunctory to permit in-depth examination of agency operations.[5]

Proposals to create programs or change agency organization also provide opportunities for oversight. When administrators seek new authority, legislators may examine whether existing authority has been used effectively and in accordance with legislative desires. Reorganization proposals may be used in a similar manner and may send signals regarding legislative preferences to administrators. Unfortunately, agencies with relatively stable programs and administrative structures create few opportunities for this type of oversight.

Individual legislators conduct oversight by contacting agencies to resolve citizen complaints and requests for assistance. This casework activity helps inform legislators and administrators of performance problems and can improve communication between legislators and administrators. Casework, however, may be biased toward paying substantial attention to problems that affect vocal, active groups and may neglect problems that are not visible to the public or that primarily affect people who are not politically active.

Probably the most spectacular form of oversight is the formal hearing or investigation. A legislative committee may summon administrators, examine agency records, and invite testimony from a variety of people from policy experts to average citizens. Agency actions may also be subjected to media exposure. A major shortcoming of formal investigations, at least in the eyes of some observers, is that formal inquiries too often occur only after a major problem is detected. Prevention seems to be an all too rare occurrence.

In spite of the many different techniques legislators have traditionally used to oversee agency operations, few observers have been satisfied with the effectiveness of legislative oversight. State legislators, with an awareness that effective legislative oversight and control are partly a function of the legislature's resources for oversight,[6] have moved in recent years to expand those resources. Longer sessions and expanded staff support mean that more time is available for oversight activities and more personnel for sharing the work. A number of legislatures have also tried to expand their capabilities by enacting sunset laws.

Sunset laws attach a fixed expiration date to government agencies and programs. When the date arrives, the agency or program ceases to exist unless the legislature enacts a new law extending the life of the agency or program, again with a fixed expiration date. Sunset laws, then, attempt to alter the agenda-setting process by creating deadlines that periodically raise the issue of whether a program, grant of authority, or agency should be retained or eliminated. Since deadlines often serve to direct attention toward the activities that have deadlines and away from activities without them,[7] sunset advocates believe that without deadlines to force action, the question of whether a particular agency or program should continue to exist is unlikely to receive adequate attention.

The ability of sunset legislation to direct attention to that question is particularly significant in view of the tendency for government agencies to survive for very long periods.[8] Agency survival is normally encouraged by a variety of factors. First, the creation of an organization typically requires the investment of substantial resources in skills and physical facilities that are difficult to transfer to other uses; the sunk costs of organization enhance its prospects for survival.[9] Second, an organization provides a variety of benefits, including agency programs, salaries, and prestige of office, all of which give people a stake in maintaining its existence.[10] The people who benefit from an agency's programs, sell supplies to an agency, or benefit from an agency's regulations are particularly powerful sources of support for many agencies.[11] In addition, organizations create emotional bonds, including pride in past achievements as well as gratitude for them and interpersonal loyalties that enhance survival prospects.[12]

Advocates of sunset laws contend that by periodically raising the issue of whether agencies should continue, the normal tendency for agencies to survive for very long periods — longer, perhaps, than necessary — can be offset to some degree. As a result, sunset legislation may help eliminate unnecessary programs, agencies, and expenditures.[13] The burden that taxpayers must bear can be correspondingly reduced.

Advocates of sunset laws also contend that such laws will stimulate program reviews that will help to make agencies more accountable and more responsive to legislative desires.[14] When an agency faces a sunset review, that agency can hardly afford to ignore legislative desires. The deadline will also force the legislature to examine agency performance, even in the face of competing demands on legislative time and energy. Moreover, a sunset review may stimulate agency personnel to improve their performance and their programs to avoid legislative displeasure.[15]

Critics of sunset laws complain that legislatures already have the authority to review program operations whenever the inclination arises. If legislators lack the inclination, sunset deadlines may simply lead to a mechanical process of filing reports that legislators ignore.[16] Other observers contend that sunset laws are of limited effectiveness for agencies with powerful clientele support; only agencies lacking such support face much risk.[17] A legislature considering elimination of the state highway program, for example, would be overwhelmed by the lobbyists representing motorists, oil companies, automobile and truck manufacturers and dealers, trucking and bus companies, and the many other groups benefiting from state support of highways.

Some observers also fear that sunset laws will play into hands of well-organized interest groups seeking to eliminate programs they oppose and legislators seeking to extract favors from agencies. An agency with well-financed, vocal opponents and weak, unorganized supporters may be undercut in spite of the benefits it produces.[18] Legislators may use the threat of program termination to pressure an agency into providing preferential treatment to favored consituents who are not the most deserving. Agencies may postpone needed actions if they are likely to generate controversy at the time of a sunset review, so that important problems are neglected.

If sunset laws carry a genuine risk of program termination, they can create other problems. The morale of public employees may decline if they are constantly fearful that their agency is going to be abolished. Private citizens may find that planning for the future is difficult when agencies and programs are frequently being abolished. Relations with other states, the national government, and local governments may be jeopardized if officials in those jurisdictions believe that a state may not be able to honor long-term commitments.

One other complication of sunset laws arises from the fact that systematic reviews of agency operations are costly and time-consuming; the costs may exceed the savings generated by program terminations and improvements.[19] If policymakers and powerful interest groups are committed to continuing a program in its present form, they may resist and even sabotage efforts to evaluate the program and ignore the results of expensive program reviews. Without some assessment of the potential market for an evaluation, substantial efforts and resources may be expended on an evaluation that no one takes seriously.[20]

While sunset legislation may have its shortcomings, then, it may still represent a significant vehicle for asserting greater legislative control over a bureaucracy. In spite of the promise of sunset legislation, however, the states have shown varying enthusiasm for sunset laws. Some states have enacted comprehensive sunset legislation; others have restricted it to certain agencies or regulations; still others have none.[21]

States with comprehensive sunset legislation were coded 2; those with limited sunset laws were coded 1; and states with no sunset provisions were coded 0.[22] The analysis will therefore be able to distinguish between a more comprehensive application of the innovation and a partial application.

Influences on Adoption

As noted in Chapter 2, a number of factors may influence adoption of policy innovations. A general tendency toward innovativeness may encourage adoption of sunset laws. Some support for this hypothesis is provided by Crane,[23] who found that extensive legislative review of programs was more likely to occur in innovative states than in laggard states. Innovativeness may stimulate legislative adoption of new methods of program review in several ways. First, an innovative state, because of its greater attentiveness to and receptivity toward new ideas, may be more willing to try a new method of program review. Second, the desire to innovate in substantive program areas may spur greater efforts at assessing old programs to determine where changes are needed. Finally, a state that changes policies more frequently may have more need for program reviews than a state that changes policies rarely. In the latter case, a proven program may require less attention than a new, untested one.[24]

The ideological environment of state policy-making may infuence adoption of sunset legislation. Ideological liberalism, with its greater emphasis on change and reform, may encourage adoption of sunset laws as yet another reform. Conservatism, with its suspicion of change, may discourage enactment of sunset legislation, particularly in a comprehensive form, because it threatens established practices and programs.

A very different possibility, however, is that conservatism may encourage adoption of sunset laws. They are regarded by many observers as devices for trimming back the size of government or slowing its growth, with similar effects on government spending.[25] Those results have traditionally been dear to the hearts of political conservatives. Conservative ideologies may therefore encourage adoption of sunset laws to control the size and cost of government. Because sunset legislation deals primarily with internal governmental relations, at least in an immediate sense, the ideological climate is probably best assessed by the ideologies of the state political parties.[26] Because of the period covered by adoptions of sunset legislation, McGregor's scales of state party ideologies will be used.[27]

While orientations toward change and the use of government power may influence adoption of sunset legislation, the availability of slack resources may also play a role. Legislative efforts at controlling state bureaucracies have long been hampered by the limited institutional resources of the state legislatures themselves. Short sessions, a lack of staff support, high turnover, and other limitations on legislative effectiveness frustrate efforts at controlling the bureaucracy. A legislature with ample time, staff support, and a corps of experienced members is far better equipped to deal with agency oversight and control.[28] Crane's analysis found that more-professionalized legislatures were more likely to engage in comprehensive program review.[29] However, Hamm and Robertson found that sunset laws were more likely to be adopted where legislative salaries were *lower*.[30] Low legislative salaries strongly limit legislative work time, for members must earn a living doing something else.

According to the slack-resources model, we would expect that more highly developed legislatures — those with longer sessions, more staff assistance, lower turnover, and reasonably organized leadership and committee structures — would be more inclined to enact sunset legislation. The more capable legislature is in a better position to carry out the evaluations which sunset laws require for maximum effectiveness. By far the most comprehensive measure of legislative capability is the FAIIR rating, which gives high ratings to state legislatures with relatively long sessions, ample staff assistance, higher salaries, better record-keeping systems, and a relatively clear and coherent organizational structure.[31]

A second aspect of the availability of slack resources is state affluence. A wealthier state is likely to have an easier time raising the funds needed to establish an analytical staff to conduct sunset reviews. A relatively poor state will generally have all its available resources committed to ongoing operations and is therefore likely to have a more-difficult time amassing the resources to support new initiatives, including sunset reviews on a large scale. In this view, affluence should encourage adoption of sunset legislation.

While inclinations toward change and the availability of slack resources may influence adoption of sunset laws, they may also be a response to the problem environment. One aspect of that environment is a lack of affluence. Legislative efforts to control the bureaucracy may be stimulated by economic scarcity.[32] When resources are abundant, political demands will be relatively easy to satisfy. With scarcity, a program needing additional resources may be able to obtain them only at the expense of other programs. Legislators may therefore increase their efforts at evaluating and paring back less-productive or lower-priority programs. According to this perspective, and contrary to the slack-resources model, poorer states should be more likely to adopt sunset laws in order to stretch limited resources as far as possible.

A second major component of the problem environment is the structure of the executive branch. In some states, the executive branch is a fragmented, dispersed collection of agencies rather than an integrated structure under the control of a strong governor. Where the executive branch fails to provide mechanisms of coordination and integrated control, legislators may feel compelled to step into the breach. Moreover, the comparatively weak governor may be less equipped to fend off legislative incursions into what the governor considers executive territory. Harris, for example, notes that in the late nineteenth century, presidents had only limited control over a bureaucracy and congressional influence was substantial.[33] Where governors are comparatively weak, then, adoption of sunset laws may be encouraged by the greater need for coordinating the executive branch and by the governors' lesser ability to stop adoption of sunset laws.

An alternative possibility, however, is that the existence of a strong governor may stimulate legislative efforts to control the bureaucracy. Wright's research found that state administrators in states with stronger governors tended to rate legislative influence as weaker than administrators in states with weak governors.[34] Moreover, administrators' perceptions of legislative and gubernatorial control indicate declining legislative influence from 1964 to 1974.[35] Legislators might respond to their limited influence over state agencies in strong-governor states by adding to the legislature's tools for overseeing the state bureaucracy.

The distribution of partisan control of state government is another important component of the problem environment. A variety of scholars have noted that legislative oversight is likely to be particularly vigilant when one party controls the legislature and the other party controls the executive.[36] In that situation, the desire to embarrass the other party may provide the stimulus to oversight. Conversely, when the governor and legislature are controlled by the same party, bonds of party loyalty and self-interest may cause legislators to avoid antagonisms with the executive branch. We would therefore expect states that experience divided control on a regular basis to be more likely to enact sunset laws, which give the legislature additional leverage on the state bureaucracy. Surprisingly, however, Hamm and Robertson found that divided control seemed to discourage adoption of sunset laws.[37] We will return to that paradoxical finding shortly.

A final aspect of the problem environment is the scope of state government. A larger bureaucracy with more money and programs is likely to affect more people and therefore to stimulate efforts at legislative control. More is at stake as government grows larger.[38] According to this perspective, the size and cost of government may provide a direct stimulus to legislative efforts to control the bureaucracy through mechanisms like sunset laws. This hypothesis is supported by Crane's analysis—which found that legislative review efforts were positively associated with state government employment, taxes, and revenue—but not by Hamm and Robertson.[39]

The scope of state government can be measured in absolute terms, relative to population, or relative to the size of the state economy. All three approaches have merit. The total size of the state budget indicates the overall magnitude of state spending and also has symbolic overtones, as in the case of the first budget in the state's history to reach a certain magnitude—the first billion-dollar budget, for example. Expenditures relative to population indicate the approximate impact of state spending per person. Expenditures relative to the size of the state economy (expenditure effort) indicate the proportional influence of state expenditures when compared to overall public and private economic activity.

An additional complication in assessing the scope of state government involves the role of local governments. In an immediate sense, legislators may be primarily concerned with government programs, a situation that would encourage measuring the scope of state government by using state-only expenditures. However, most state programs are jointly administered with local governments, and the states have many powers for influencing local governments.[40] In this view, combined state-local expenditures may provide more valid information regarding the scope of state government activity. Because of the uncertainty regarding the most appropriate measures of government activity, subsequent analysis will include a variety of measures, including state-only and state-local spending in absolute terms as well as relative to the state population and size of the state economy.

Analysis

The findings presented in Table 5.1 provide some support for the preceding hypotheses, but also some surprises. States with a history of being quick to adopt innovations are *less* likely to have adopted sunset

TABLE 5.1. ■ Influences on enactment of sunset laws

	Sunset laws[a]
Innovation (Walker, 1969)	−.26[c]
Republican ideology (McGregor, 1978)	−.20
Democratic ideology (McGregor, 1978)	.29[c]
FAIIR ranking (*Report,* 1971)	.30
Median income, 1975	−.30[c]
Governors' powers (Rosenthal, 1981: 237)	−.38[d]
Divided control, 1971−80[b]	−.36[d]
State-local expenditures, 1977 (total)	−.27[c]
State-local expenditures per capita, 1977	−.36[e]
State-local expenditure effort, 1977	−.28[c]
State expenditures (total), 1977	−.22
State expenditures per capita, 1977	−.10
State expenditure effort, 1977	−.15

[a]Coded as follows: 2 = comprehensive; 1 = limited; 0 = none.

[b]For each biennium, if the governor and both houses of the legislature are controlled by the same party, score is 0. If governor's party controls only one house, score is $1/2$. If governor's party controls neither house, score is 1. Scores for each biennium are totaled for 1971 through 1980.

[c]Significant at the .05 level; correlations are Pearson's r's.

[d]Significant at the .01 level.

[e]Significant at the .001 level.

laws than other states. States adopting sunset laws tend to have relatively conservative Democratic parties, as would be expected if sunset laws were viewed as a method for reducing the size and cost of government. In short, sunset laws tend to be found in relatively conservative states that are normally slow to adopt new programs.

The slack-resources model is substantially contradicted by the data. Sunset laws tend to be found in states with low legislative salaries, short legislative sessions, little legislative staff support, and otherwise weak legislatures (high scores on the FAIIR ranking indicate a relatively weak legislature). In addition, states adopting sunset laws tend to be relatively poor. In spite of the added costs of sunset reviews, then, states that are more likely to have slack resources are *not* more likely to adopt sunset laws. The opposite tendency occurs.

The hypothesis that sunset laws are a response to the problem environment receives mixed support at the zero-order level. As noted previously, poorer states, which are under more pressure to stretch their limited resources as far as possible, are more likely to adopt sunset laws than wealthier states. In addition, states with relatively weak governors, who are likely to have difficulty controlling the executive branch and difficulty in fending off legislative efforts to control the bureaucracy, are more likely to adopt sunset laws.

Contrary to the problem-environment hypothesis, however, sunset laws tend to be found in states with a recent history of unified partisan control of the governor and legislature. Moreover, states with sunset laws tend to have relatively low levels of state-local spending in the period preceding virtually all the sunset reviews. The laws do not appear to be a legislative response to divided partisan control or unusually high public spending.

Overall, the zero-order relationships for sunset legislation contradict some of the hypotheses but form a generally consistent pattern. Sunset laws are more common in states with low legislative capability, weak governors, a reluctance to adopt innovations, conservative Democratic parties, and low expenditures — in short, an apparently negative orientation toward government. States with more positive orientations toward government — as indicated by well-developed legislative and gubernatorial institutions, a history of innovativeness, liberal Democratic parties, and higher state-local expenditures — tend not to have sunset laws.

A multivariate analysis of state sunset laws indicates that they can be explained to a significant degree by the extent of divided partisan control and gubernatorial powers.[41] As at the zero-order level, states with sunset laws tend to have a recent history of unified partisan control and governors with relatively weak formal powers. None of the other predictors examined in this analysis could significantly improve the fit of the model (see Table 5.2).

TABLE 5.2. ■ Regression analysis of state sunset legislation

	Beta
Extent of divided control	−.28[a]
Governor's powers	−.30[a]
Multiple R = .46	
R^2 = .21	
N = 47	

[a]Significant at the .05 level.

The multivariate findings, viewed in the context of the zero-order results, indicate that sunset laws are more likely in states with a negative orientation toward government, as indicated by the formal powers of the governor. Unified partisan control also improves the prospects for adoption, perhaps because enacting an innovation is likely to be easier in a context of unified partisan control, particularly when the innovation may have implications for legislative-gubernatorial relations. The overall predictive power of the multivariate analysis is not impressive, however.

Conclusions

The preceding analysis indicates that sunset laws have been most widely adopted in states with a relatively negative orientation to government. The weak legislatures and governors, conservative Democratic parties, reluctance to innovate, and low levels of expenditure in the sunset-law states all reflect that negative orientation. The negative relationships between adoption of sunset laws on one hand and legislative capabilities and state wealth on the other contradict the slack-innovation hypothesis but support Aberbach's contention that resource scarcity may stimulate oversight activity.[42] Because sunset reviews can be scheduled to correspond to very short legislative sessions and can be quite elaborate or very simple, sunset laws may be manageable for the least capable of state legislatures.

The institutional, ideological, and expenditure patterns are consistent with the contention that sunset laws reflect a generally negative orientation toward government. While some advocates contend that sunset laws can play a positive role in stimulating accountability and responsiveness,[43] the fundamental assumption in sunset legislation is that some programs and agencies are unnecessary and should be terminated. It is therefore a basically negative orientation toward the state bureaucracy, both in principle and in terms of the states likely to have it.

The tendency for sunset laws to be found in states with relatively unified partisan control of the governorship and legislature is strongly inconsistent with the general view that divided partisan control stimulates oversight activity. However, the unexpected findings regarding partisan control are interpretable in light of the findings regarding orientations toward government power. If sunset laws are a reflection of frictions between elected officials and public bureaucracies[44] rather than between governor and legislature, then unified partisan control of the executive and legislative branches may facilitate translation of the frictions between elected officials and bureaucrats into a tangible form such as a sunset law.

NOTES

See Bibliography for full reference.

1. Grant and Omdahl (1987: 198–194); Rosenthal (1981: chapters 12–14).
2. Keefe and Ogul (1985: 333).
3. Keefe and Ogul (1985: 332); Rosenthal (1981: 314).
4. Keefe and Ogul (1985: 334–350); Rosenthal (1981: 316–329).
5. See Anton (1966).

6. Ogul (1976: 11–13).
7. March and Simon (1958: 185); Walker (1977: 424–425).
8. Kaufman (1976).
9. March and Simon (1958: 173); Presthus (1978: 253, 257).
10. Kaufman (1976: 9–10); Starbuck (1965: 471).
11. Rourke (1984: 48–90).
12. Barnard (1938: 251–252); Kaufman (1976: 9–10).
13. Nigro and Nigro (1980: 460); Rosenthal (1981: 322–323).
14. Kopel (1976: 138); Shimberg (1976: 145).
15. Pound (1982: 183).
16. Press and VerBurg (1983: 367).
17. Fesler (1980: 329–330); Maddox and Fuguay (1981: 75).
18. Nigro and Nigro (1980: 461); Fiorina (1981: 337); Ethridge (1981).
19. Pound (1982: 183).
20. See Rossi and Freeman (1982: 74).
21. *Book of the States* (1980: 120–124).
22. Comprehensive provisions include all state agencies. Limited sunset laws cover only some agencies.
23. Crane (1977: 177).
24. This is not to say that noninnovative states have an array of programs that have proven excellent but that more frequent changes in programs may call for more program review efforts, other things being equal.
25. Nigro and Nigro (1980: 460); Rosenthal (1981: 317).
26. A study of constituency voting on referenda and state legislator's voting behavior in Iowa revealed that constitutency voting was very weakly related to legislative voting on proposals to give the governor an item veto and to establish annual legislative sessions, the issues most similar to sunset laws (see Friesema and Hedlund, 1981).
27. McGregor (1978: 1020–1023).
28. Jewell (1969: 128); Keefe (1966: 47); Rosenthal (1981: 315– 316).
29. Crane (1977: 102).
30. Hamm and Robertson (1981: 144–146).
31. *Report on an Evaluation of the 50 State Legislatures* (1971: 29).
32. Aberbach (1979: 499).
33. Harris (1964: 281–282).
34. Wright (1967).
35. Keefe and Ogul (1985: 356–357).
36. Harris (1964: 280); Ogul (1976: 18); Scher (1963); Simon, Smithburg, and Thompson (1950: 525).
37. Hamm and Robertson (1981: 144–147).
38. Keefe and Ogul (1985: 332–333); Scher (1963).
39. Compare Crane (1977: 95) and Hamm and Robertson (1981).
40. Glendening and Reeves (1984: 131–158); Nice (1987c: 137–148).
41. The three-level sunset legislation variable is a somewhat marginal candidate for regression analysis. However, regression analysis is not very sensitive to violations of its assumptions regarding the dependent variable (see Bohrnstedt and Knoke [1982: 231], Kerlinger and Pedhazur [1973: 47–48]). In addition, more conservative analytical techniques produce very similar results (Nice, 1985b).
42. Aberbach (1979: 499).
43. Kopel (1976); Shimberg (1976).
44. For discussions of those frictions, see Lowi (1968) and Lipsky (1980).

Public Financing of Election Campaigns

Introduction

Campaigning for public office in the United States is increasingly expensive. In 1952, the costs of all election campaigns amounted to approximately $140 million. By 1980, the combined costs of all campaigns reached $1.2 billion, more than double the total of just four years earlier. The advent of new campaign techniques, including television advertising, public opinion polling, and computerized mailings, have made running for office a costly business and created a significant industry of media consultants, pollsters, and other providers of campaign assistance. The costs of campaigns for state offices alone surpassed the quarter-billion-dollar mark in 1980.[1] Candidates for public office find that attracting campaign contributions to pay for the new technologies now constitutes a major portion of the campaign, at least for major offices.

Technological changes are not the only causes of rising campaign costs. Many candidates find that a personal campaign organization must be created to win the party nomination; once that organization is created, the typical candidate is often inclined to stay with the proven approach. Moreover, party organizations in many areas are too feeble to carry on a campaign entirely on their own. Candidates who need to reach voters of the other party or voters who have no party affiliation may regard a personal organization as a more appropriate campaign vehicle than a political party. The personal organization cannot function without considerable sums of money.

A large campaign treasury is also a fairly effective way to scare off potential opponents. An elected official who has amassed a substantial sum of money well before the next campaign begins is a formidable adversary or will at least give that impression. Incumbents, therefore, devote considerable attention to fund-raising and typically discover that many groups are more than willing to make a contribution. Challengers who face those incumbents feel a need for similarly large treasuries; higher campaign spending results.

The escalating cost of campaigns has highlighted a long-standing tension between two forms of political participation, voting and contributing money to campaigns. In voting, assuming sufficient motivation and honest administration, citizens participate on reasonably equal terms with one another.[2] In campaign contributions, however, affluent people and organizations may be able to exert much greater influence than those with modest means.[3] A millionaire or interest group with a large bankroll can afford to give thousands of dollars to a single candidate; a worker earning the minimum wage cannot. Contributing money is therefore a form of participation that may give some people much more political influence than others. A policy innovation designed to reduce the presumed inequality of influence is public funding of election campaigns.

The importance of money in politics stems from its value as a political resource that presumably benefits candidates who have it in abundance.[4] Unlike some other political resources, money can easily be moved from one location or jurisdiction to another, can sometimes be given without revealing the source's identity, and can easily be converted into other types of political resources, such as information, visibility, and labor.[5] However, money is only one resource of many. Partisan loyalties, issues, incumbency, and many other factors may offset a candidate's advantage in campaign funds. Abundant funds will be of little help if they are expended on unproductive activities.[6] A candidate who spends large sums on boring, offensive, or confusing advertisements may lose rather than gain support. A high-priced campaign consultant may add substantial costs while producing few useful ideas. Poorly attended campaign appearances will drain the travel budget but reach few people.

A number of recent studies have explored the relationship between campaign expenditures and electoral outcomes.[7] Collectively, the literature supports the contention that money is a significant resource, although its influence varies from candidate to candidate.

Some research has found that campaign spending by challengers in legislative elections has more impact on election results than spending by incumbents.[8] Apparently, the challengers, who in many cases are not well known, need ample campaign budgets to achieve visibility, become recognized, and build campaign organizations. Incumbents are likely to be well known and have an organization already in place. They use the conduct of office to build support and spend more when in electoral difficulty. When they face strong opponents, however, incumbents also benefit from higher campaign outlays.[9]

Some studies indicate that campaign spending is more productive for Republicans than Democrats.[10] One explanation for that tendency is the Republican party's smaller base of supporters. Lacking the Democratic party's larger group of relatively loyal identifiers, Republican candidates may be more dependent on campaign expenditures for mobilizing support. A second explanation is that Democratic candidates may place more reliance on nonmonetary contributions, particularly volunteer labor.[11] Consequently, expenditures may indicate less about the resource bases of Democratic candidates. A third explanation lies in the Democratic party's inclusive coalitional strategy,[12] which involves distributing government aid or benefits to many groups. That strategy lends itself well to campaigning on the basis of distributing benefits, especially for incumbents. Because Republicans are less inclined to support government assistance of various kinds, they may be more dependent on campaign spending as a means of mobilizing electoral support.[13]

Campaign spending may be subject to the law of diminishing returns.[14] Beyond some point, additional expenditures grow less and less productive, apparently because effective activities reach the saturation point and funds are increasingly devoted to marginal and even unproductive uses. After a campaign has reached relatively open-minded people and mobilized supporters, additional spending will largely involve preaching to the already converted or appealing to people who are committed opponents. Neither effort will alter the election's outcome very much.

Overall, the literature indicates that campaign expenditures do influence election outcomes, at least in some instances. Consequently, people who are able to contribute substantial sums to election campaigns are able to engage in an effective form of political participation that is not open to other people. However, political money is not always particularly influential. As noted earlier, many factors besides campaign spending affect election outcomes. In addition, money tends to gravitate to candidates who are expected to do well.[15] Contributors who give to gain a sympathetic hearing from elected officials tend to channel contributions to likely winners; in that situation, an assurance of victory leads to a large campaign budget rather than vice versa.

Sources of Worry

The practices associated with campaign finance in the United States have been a source of concern for some observers for years. The escalating cost of campaigns has been a source of worry.[16] Critics have complained that candidates are unduly vulnerable to influence by major campaign contributors and must sometimes resort to exchanges of political favors to raise necessary campaign funds.[17] When huge sums are commonplace in campaigns, powerful temptations result. Not everyone can resist the allure of hundreds of thousands of dollars.

The growing role of political action committees, or PACs, in financing candidate campaigns and financing "independent" campaigns, which are officially separate from the campaigns of declared candidates, has raised further concerns regarding undue political influence. Not all observers share the view that PACs are excessively powerful or dangerous. But there is little doubt that PACs are raising and spending substantial sums in an effort to influence election outcomes and cultivate goodwill among public officials. In the process, viewpoints not represented by PACs may receive proportionally less attention.[18]

Concerns regarding campaign spending were heightened by the U.S. Supreme Court's ruling in *Buckley* v. *Valeo*. The court ruled that spending money to publicize one's beliefs was a form of free speech protected by the Constitution. A candidate can therefore spend an unlimited sum of his or her own money in pursuit of public office. In addition, individuals and groups can spend unlimited sums to publicize their beliefs, including beliefs regarding candidates for public office, as long as those activities are not officially coordinated with any candidate's campaign.[19] The *Buckley* decision has given considerable freedom to people and groups with large bankrolls and an interest in election outcomes.

More generally, the fact that some people and organizations can afford to contribute thousands of dollars to campaigns while other people and groups cannot may cause public officials to pay undue attention to contributors and potential contributors and to neglect people who cannot afford to give. The Declaration of Independence's professed belief in equality is undermined by the unequal ability to exert influence through political money. Because the states have major responsibilities in administering and regulating elections, questions regarding inequality in campaign finance have faced many state officials.

Political Equality

State governments make many policies affecting the equality or in-equality of their citizens. States may adopt tax and expenditure policies that redistribute income from rich to poor or may leave the existing distribution of income relatively intact.[20] Some states moved to give black Americans legal equality prior to federal efforts. Other states adopted laws requiring racial discrimination and fought efforts to pro-mote racial equality.[21] Some states have approved giving women consti-tutional equality; others have vacillated; still others have opposed it.[22]

In the realm of political equality, many states failed to provide their citizens with equal political influence in legislative elections. Malappor-tionment had the effect of making some citizens' votes more powerful than others.[23] Some states have made access to the ballot box relatively easy, and others have made it comparatively difficult and inconvenient.[24]

The states also affect political equality by making policies regarding campaign finance.[25] Limitations on the size of contributions can restrict the influence wielded by concentrated wealth and encourage broader citizen participation in campaign finance through increasing reliance on small donations. Limitations on giving by corporations and political-action committees appear particularly significant in that regard, for they have economic resources far beyond individual citizen's.[26]

In a similar vein, public finance of campaigns reduces the influence wealthy individuals and organizations can exert in a system of private finance.[27] Public funding reduces dependence on private contributors and therefore frees candidates to pay more attention to the electorate as a whole. Public finance through income tax–checkoff systems also broadens the base of political contributors by attracting "contributions" from people who would not otherwise give funds to candidates.[28]

The adoption of public finance of state election campaigns[29] was stimulated in part by the financial scandals associated with Watergate.[30] The state programs are typically modest; they generally cover only a limited number of offices and frequently pay only a fraction of total campaign costs.[31] Nevertheless, public finance of state campaigns repre-sents an interesting case of a policy innovation with potentially signifi-cant consequences for the careers of the policymakers who adopt it. Even a limited system of public finance represents a gesture toward political equality.[32] Data on state public finance programs is from the *Book of the States*.[33]

Influences on Adoption of Public Financing

A variety of factors may influence whether state campaign finance laws provide public funding. Ideological-cultural factors are likely to shape adoption. Cultural norms may place a high value on equality and encourage government action to promote it. The "moralistic" political culture, with its emphasis on the public good, its view that people should not gain economically from political involvement, and its belief in government as an instrument to promote the public good,[34] is likely to encourage the adoption of public financing. Predominantly moralistic states are coded 2; secondarily moralistic states are coded 1; other states are coded 0.

Elazar's other two political cultures appear likely to discourage adoption of publicly financed campaigns, but for different reasons. The "individualistic" political culture, with its emphasis on private rather than public concerns and its view of politics as a quasi marketplace in which people can advance socially and economically,[35] is likely to discourage adoption of policies that hamper individual efforts at influencing the government or moving upward. Public financing, with its corresponding reduction in candidate reliance on substantial individual and group contributions, reduces the opportunities for exerting individual influence through those contributions. That result is not consistent with the individualistic culture.

The "traditionalistic" political culture, which is elitist and seeks to maintain the existing social order, partly by confining political power to a small group,[36] is unlikely to favor limiting the influence of affluent citizens and groups. Publicly financed campaigns reduce the control affluent citizens and groups exert over campaign finance and consequently threaten elite control. Candidates who are hostile to traditional elites may have greater prospects for victory under public finance, and the reduced opportunities for cultivating goodwill among elected officials by contributing to their campaigns may also reduce elite influence. Overall, cultural traditionalism is likely to discourage adoption.

In a related vein, party ideology may influence a state's orientation toward public funding. Political conservatives, with their suspicion of change, reluctance to use government to change society, and reservations regarding equality, are likely to oppose government efforts to increase political equality through publicly financed campaigns. Liberals, who tend to be more open to innovation, experimentation, and change; more supportive of equality; and more willing to use government as an instrument of social change, are likely to support efforts at equalizing influence in campaign finance. Liberals are likely to be more supportive of both the end and the means of publicly subsidizing campaigns. Party ideology is particularly relevant because decisions regarding campaign finance have significant implications for party politics in relationships between the parties and internal party politics.[37]

Because public financing is a comparatively new idea, some states may not have gone that far in support of political equality because of their general reluctance to do new things. Previous experience with innovation may be especially important for reforms like public financing, which represents a drastic (at the symbolic level at least) departure from the traditional, long-established practice of privately financed campaigns. A history of innovativeness should foster adoption of public finance.

While political factors may influence a state's response to campaign finance policy, economic and social factors may also play key roles, as they do in many aspects of state policy-making. A state that is financially hard pressed may be less willing to commit scarce funds to public finance of campaigns when long-standing programs are clamoring for money. Prosperity may encourage state officials to commit funds to what may otherwise seem a low-priority need (in contrast to education, welfare, transportation, and other programs). Slack resources, then, may encourage innovation.

Education levels may influence campaign finance policy. Public opinion research has found a general tendency for more highly educated people to express more support for equality (on noneconomic issues) and to be more supportive of equal political rights for blacks and women.[38] That support could provide a more receptive climate for efforts to promote political equality in the realm of campaign finance through mechanisms like public financing.

Public officials are likely to regard the problem environment in campaign finance in terms of career interests. As noted earlier, some research indicates that campaign spending is particularly helpful for Republican candidates. A system of public funding of campaigns could reduce the ability of Republican candidates to outspend their Democratic opponents. As a result, Republican dominance is likely to reduce the odds of enacting public financing. The problem environment in this case, is the distribution of party strength, which in turn reflects the career concerns of elected officials.

Analysis

The zero-order relationships between state characteristics and adoption of public financing are consistent with only some of the preceding hypotheses. The most substantial relationships indicate that states with more moralistic cultures and more liberal Republican parties are more likely to adopt public funding (see Table 6.1). The moralistic culture, with its emphasis on active government and "clean," honest politics,[39] provides a more supportive environment for public funding. In a similar vein, more liberal Republican ideologies, with their greater emphasis on equality and government activism, are likely to be more supportive of public funding.

TABLE 6.1. ■ State characteristics and public finance of campaigns

	Public funding
Degree of moralism	.26[a]
Republican Ideology[b] (McGregor, 1978)	.27
Democratic Ideology[c] (McGregor, 1978)	−.11
Innovation Score[d] (Walker, 1969)	.20
Median income	.14
Percent high school graduates	.09
Republican dominance	.10

[a]Coefficients are Pearson's r's. States with public funding are coded 1; other states are coded 0.
[b]High scores indicate liberalism.
[c]High scores indicate conservatism.
[d]High scores indicate high innovativeness.

Contrary to expectations, however, Democratic ideology is essentially unrelated to adoption. States with a history of being quick to adopt new programs are more likely to adopt public financing as expected, but the tendency is comparatively weak. Wealthier and better-educated states are more likely to enact public financing, as hypothesized, but both relationships are very weak. Finally, Republican dominance (calculated by subtracting the Ranney index of party balance from 1)[40] is of almost no value in accounting for adoption of public financing at the zero-order level.

Discriminant analysis of public financing produces a model that

reflects the two strongest bivariate relationships but also reveals an interaction effect consistent with other research on party differences in campaign spending (see Table 6.2).[41] States with more moralistic political
cultures are more likely to enact public financing, as expected. States
with more liberal Republican parties are also more likely to adopt public
funding systems, but an interaction effect is also present. Simply put, the
interaction effect indicates that under conditions of Republican dominance, Republican party liberalism does not promote enactment of public finance of campaigns. The model is able to predict the decisions of
nearly three fourths of the states.

TABLE 6.2. ■ Discriminant analysis of public finance of state campaigns

	Standardized canonical discriminant function coefficients	
Degree of moralism	1.21	
Republican ideology	2.04	
Republican ideology times Republican dominance	−2.32	
Canonical correlation	.53	Group centroids[a]
Wilks's lambda	.72	Group 0 − .42
Chi^2 (significant at .002 level with 3 d.f.)	14.91	Group 1 .92
Percent correctly classified	72.92	

[a]Group 0: State does not have public finance. Group 1: State has public finance.

The interaction effect is intuitively reasonable in light of two basic
facts of political finance. First, as noted earlier, Republican candidates'
performances seem to be particularly affected by how much they spend.
Second, people tend to contribute more to candidates who appear likely
to win. In a state where the Republican party is relatively dominant,
Republican candidates will have an easy time raising funds and will be
substantially helped as a result. To enact a system of public funding in
that situation would be to vote away a major partisan advantage — something few prudent politicians would do regardless of ideology or party
affiliation.

Conclusions

The states vary considerably in their enthusiasm for political equality. Over the years, citizens in some states were equally represented in
their state legislatures, while citizens in other states were not. Some
states made efforts to grant political equality to blacks, while other states
strained in the opposite direction. The states have disagreed on the question of equal rights for women. As this analysis indicates, the states have

shown different degrees of support for political equality in financing election campaigns.

State responses to political equality in campaign financing reflect cultural and ideological forces as well as considerations of partisan advantage. Where political cultures and Republican ideologies support government activism, equality, and the concept of a public good, states are more likely to enact public financing. However, Republican party dominance tends to blunt the impact of Republican ideology, a finding consistent with the view that public officials are sensitive to the career implications of their decisions.[42] Under conditions of Republican party dominance, Republican candidates are likely to be relatively successful in raising campaign funds and likely to benefit at the polls. Public financing in that context is likely to receive a cool reception.

The results of this analysis should not obscure the fact that all the states remain a substantial distance from perfect equality in the realm of campaign finance. The finance systems currently in effect fail to cover many offices and generally cover only a small share of campaign costs. The limited scope of existing programs may help to explain the weak performance of the slack-innovation hypothesis. A limited system of public funding is probably within the financial reach of any state, and there is not much evidence of movement to expand existing programs. As the impact of Watergate fades, the enactment of more comprehensive systems appears unlikely. The tension between equality at the ballot box and inequality in campaign finance is likely to remain for the foreseeable future.

Indeed, some observers regard inequality as an inescapable fact of political life. People who are interested in politics are likely to be better informed than people who find politics boring and ignore it. Some candidates are photogenic and have pleasant-sounding voices; candidates who lack those qualities may be seriously hampered in increasingly television-oriented campaigns. Some would-be candidates are born with famous names that give them a significant edge over more obscure rivals. In these and countless other ways, some people have significant advantages in the political arena, advantages that cannot be legislated away.

History provides many examples of innovations that helped promote political equality, however. Expansions of the suffrage, direct election of U.S. senators, the democratization of the electoral college, the direct primary, the secret ballot, and redistricting of state legislatures all helped to equalize political influence. Public financing of campaigns emerges as yet another innovation designed to increase political equality.

NOTES

See Bibliography for full reference.

1. Alexander (1984: 8–10).

2. Strictly speaking, the American electoral system reveals a number of deviations from the ideal of all votes being equally influential. During malapportionment, some voters were clearly more influential that others. The U.S. Senate magnifies the influence of voters in small states. The electoral college produces less than perfect equality among voters. A lack of effective interparty competition decreases the value of votes in comparison with more competitive settings (Schattschneider, 1960: 80). With these qualifications, however, voting remains a relatively equalitarian form of participation for those who are willing to participate.

3. Adamany and Agree (1975: 2); Alexander (1980: 1); Dunn (1972: 140).

4. Adamany (1972: 1–4); Alexander (1972: 37, 39).

5. Adamany and Agree (1975: 3).

6. Dunn (1972: 3–8).

7. Glantz, Abramowitz, and Burkart (1976); Green and Krasno (1988); Jacobson (1980); Nice (1987d); Welch (1976).

8. Jacobson (1980: 41–44); Glantz, Abramowitz, and Burkart (1976).

9. Green and Krasno (1988).

10. Jacobson (1980: 45–58); Nice (1987d); Welch (1976: 351).

11. Sorauf (1980: 309).

12. Mayhew (1966: 147–168).

13. Nice (1987d).

14. Caldeira and Patterson (1982); Nice (1987d); Welch (1976).

15. Jacobson (1980); Jacobson and Kernell (1981); Wayne (1980).

16. Alexander (1984: 8–15).

17. Alexander (1984: 65–66).

18. See Alexander (1984: 88–108), Fleischmann and Nice (1988), Sabato (1984), and Malbin (1980: 152–184) for varying assessments of PACs.

19. For an overview of the *Buckley* decision, see Alexander (1984: 38–42, 126, 138–141).

20. DeLeon (1973); Booms and Halldorson (1973).

21. Dye (1981: 367–384).

22. Dye (1981: 84–86); Nice (1986).

23. Dye (1981: 129–134); Grant and Nixon (1982: 225–238).

24. Kim, Petrocik, and Enokson (1975).

25. For general overviews of state regulation of campaign finance, see Alexander (1984: chapter 7) and Jones (1980, 1981).

26. Alexander (1976: 5).

27. Alexander (1976: 1, 8); Jones (1980: 283).

28. Jones (1980: 295).

29. The states with public finance of campaigns as of August 1981 (*Book of the States,* 1982: 103) were Hawaii, Idaho, Iowa, Kentucky, Maine, Maryland, Massachusetts, Michigan, Minnesota, Montana, New Jersey, North Carolina, Oklahoma, Rhode Island, Utah, and Wisconsin.

30. Sorauf (1984: 336).

31. Fling (1979: 256–257); Jones (1980: 286–290).

32. As with all official policies, the results of campaign finance policies may not always reflect the apparent inclinations of the policy. State enforcement of campaign

finance laws has generally been hampered by limited staff and funding (Alexander, 1980: 134–135; Fling, 1979: 261–262).

33. *Book of the States* (1982: 103).

34. Elazar (1972: 96–98).

35. Elazar (1972: 94).

36. Elazar (1972: 99).

37. See Jones (1981).

38. Erikson, Luttbeg, and Tedin (1980: 158–165); Pierce, Beatty, and Hagner (1982: 268, 278).

39. Nice (1983b); Peters and Welch (1978).

40. Ranney (1976: 61).

41. When the states that use a tax add-on for their public finance systems are excluded (Maine, Maryland, Massachusetts, Montana), the results of the discriminant analysis are virtually identical to those in Table 6.2. All of the variables in Table 6.1 were eligible for inclusion in the model. Tests for an interaction effect generated by Democratic party ideology and Democratic party dominance revealed no interaction effect.

42. See Mayhew (1974).

7

Rail Passenger Service

Introduction

Transportation consistently ranks as one of the most important responsibilities of state governments. Transportation programs, education, welfare, and health make up the four largest items in the typical state budget. Total state spending on transportation has exceeded $20 billion annually since 1980.[1] Transportation programs provide employment for many people, both in building and maintaining transportation systems such as highways and airports and companies that use those facilities, companies such as the airlines and trucking businesses.

Transportation systems also have longer-run consequences for state economies. Improvements in transportation facilities can help to stimulate the state's economy.[2] Few industries are likely to locate or expand in areas where raw materials cannot be readily brought in or finished products cannot be economically shipped to waiting customers. Inconvenient, unreliable, or overly expensive transportation systems will cause potential tourists to take their business elsewhere.

Transportation has many other important implications for a state and its residents. A poorly designed highway system will produce many traffic deaths and injuries. A busy airport located near residential areas will create major noise problems. Systems that cannot function in poor weather may leave residents unable to reach schools, hospitals, or other vital services. The functioning of a state's transportation system helps to determine whether travel, for business or recreation, is an enjoyable experience or an ordeal.

The Railroads

While the main emphasis of state transportation programs in recent years has been roads and highways, the states have a long history of shaping the development and operation of all aspects of the nation's transportation system, including the railroads. During the 1800s, when many states lacked rail service, they adopted a variety of subsidy programs to encourage expansion of the railroads. Land grants, tax exemptions, bond guarantees, stock purchases, and donations of cash and securities were used to bring rail service to particular areas.[3]

As the railroads expanded, new problems emerged. Many areas had no developed transportation except a single railroad, a situation that led to pricing abuses. The wealth the railroads generated and the ethics of some railroad magnates led to political corruption and financial misconduct. Railroad accidents heightened concerns about public safety. The states responded with a variety of railroad regulations in the late 1800s.[4]

A noticeable aspect of the railroad issue in recent years has been the declining availability of passenger rail service. In 1939, passenger trains provided 8 percent of all intercity passenger miles and two thirds of the intercity passenger miles on public carriers. By 1983, their contributions had fallen to 0.7 percent and 4 percent, respectively.[5] The United States had approximately 20,000 passenger trains at the beginning of the Great Depression but fewer than 500 by 1970.[6] Private passenger service lost hundreds of millions of dollars annually during the 1950s and 1960s,[7] and the nation's railroads grew increasingly unwilling, and in some cases financially unable, to sustain those losses.

With the United States facing the probable extinction of passenger service, the national government created Amtrak to ensure that service on major corridors would be maintained and to improve the quality of service on routes that still had passenger trains.[8] The legislation creating Amtrak provided that states not receiving as much service as their citizens or officials desire have the option of enacting subsidies to induce Amtrak to provide services not otherwise available. The state role is significant because some of the effects of transportation, such as influence on economic flows, are localized and effects that might seem minor from a national perspective may be very important from a state perspective.[9] State participation can help to ensure that those localized effects are beneficial. As of April 1985, nine states provided subsidies to Amtrak, while the other thirty-nine of the contiguous forty-eight did not. The subsidizing states included California, Florida, Illinois, Michigan, Minnesota, Missouri, New York, North Carolina, and Pennsylvania.[10]

The analysis that follows will seek to explain why some states subsidize Amtrak while others do not.

Government subsidies for individual transportation have generally been justified on two grounds. First, if some modes are subsidized while others are not, substantial distortions will result unless the differential treatment is based on some compelling rationale.[11] Second, subsidies may be needed if a transportation mode produces externalities, whether in the form of indirect economic benefits to nonusers or noneconomic benefits.[12]

The existence of substantial government subsidies for air and road-based transportation modes,[13] according to the first justification, may be grounds for subsidizing rail service. When governments at all levels spend billions of dollars annually on road and highway programs and substantial sums to support air travel, passenger trains are likely to have great difficulty surviving without similar support.

Alternatively, externalities arising from transportation decisions could provide grounds for subsidy. One of the most-compelling externalities involves the effects of transportation decisions on national security.[14] The current pattern of individual transportation decisions and government policies has produced a transportation system overwhelmingly dependent on petroleum fuels.[15] As a result, the United States is significantly dependent on imported petroleum and is vulnerable to interruptions in supplies, a situation that led one group of analysts to describe America's energy dependence as an "Achilles' heel."[16] The volume of U.S. oil imports also limits the import options of other nations, some of which currently have few alternatives to trading with oil-producing countries that are politically unstable or hostile to U.S. interests.

The petroleum demands generated by the transportation system, which accounts for roughly half of all U.S. petroleum consumption,[17] caused a substantial decline in U.S. petroleum reserves. Proven U.S. reserves fell every year from 1970 to 1982, a total decline of approximately 33 percent.[18] In view of the enormous petroleum demands of a full-scale military mobilization, the dwindling of domestic reserves is grounds for concern. Moreover, a full-scale mobilization, with its accompanying high petroleum requirements, would leave the current domestic transportation system seriously impaired. Rail transportation, whether with electrified track or a new generation of coal-powered locomotives,[19] can provide mobility for passengers and freight without oil-based fuels.

Other externalities generated by transportation decisions affect the use of land. Automobile-based transportation requires extensive space, which takes land out of production of food.[20] The automobile is the most dangerous of the major transportation modes,[21] and the costs of deaths and injuries are shifted in part to other people through such mechanisms as life insurance, private health insurance, Social Security, Medicare, and Medicaid. A transportation system also shapes the flow of commerce; businesses that depend on tourists, for example, will be profoundly affected by transportation changes that reduce the influx of potential customers. Collectively, those externalities provide a basis for public subsidy of transportation programs.

Influences on Subsidization

As noted earlier, ideological forces may shape the adoption of policy innovations. Although interest-group politics is a major factor in many transportation decisions,[22] ideological factors may also influence transportation policies.[23] Where political values emphasize individualism and the virtues of private-sector decision making, government intervention in what are viewed as market decisions is likely to be discouraged.[24] The extensive government involvement in transportation makes it a far cry from a free market, but market forces do operate to some degree, and the emphasis on private-sector decision making receives substantial support in many circles. Liberals, with their greater willingness to use government to attack social problems, might see passenger rail service as a means of promoting public health and safety. For example, available evidence clearly indicates that train travel is far safer than travel by automobile.[25]

Analysis reveals that states with more liberal electorates are considerably more likely to subsidize Amtrak than states with relatively conservative electorates (see Table 7.1). Slightly more than one third of the states that gave 38 percent or more of their popular vote to George McGovern in the 1972 presidential election subsidize Amtrak, but only two of the twenty-eight states that gave less support to McGovern subsidize passenger service. In a similar fashion, states with more conservative electorates, as measured by pooled estimates from public opinion polls, are clearly less likely to subsidize Amtrak. Both measures of electoral ideology, then, indicate that liberalism encourages subsidization.

While the ideological leanings of state electorates may shape state policy decisions, party ideologies also influence some policy decisions. To the degree that substantial policy changes require organized political influence rather than just unorganized public sentiment, the ideological inclinations of the parties may play a crucial role.

TABLE 7.1. ■ Electoral liberalism and Amtrak subsidy

		Percent for McGovern, 1972[a]			
		38% or more		37% or less	
Amtrak	Yes	35%	(7)	7%	(2)
subsidy	No	65	(13)	93	(26) (gamma = .75)

		Survey estimates of state electoral ideology[b]			
		.144 or higher		.141 or lower	
Amtrak	Yes	8%	(2)	30%	(7)
subsidy	No	92	(23)	70	(16) (gamma = −.67)

NOTE: Amtrak subsidy information is from *Amtrak National Train Timetables,* April 28, 1985.

[a]*Congressional Quarterly Almanac* (1972: 1014); Alaska and Hawaii omitted from this and all subsequent analyses.

[b]Wright, Erickson, and McIver (1985: 478–480); high scores indicate conservatism; coefficients are unweighted, and the corrected value for Nevada is used.

As Table 7.2 indicates, party ideologies appear to be less influential than public views in shaping Amtrak subsidy decisions. States with more liberal Republican parties are more likely to subsidize Amtrak, as expected, but the relationship is not terribly strong. Moreover, Democratic party ideology is essentially unrelated to subsidy decisions. Overall, the evidence indicates that if ideological forces shape the adoption of Amtrak subsidies, the broad views of the public seem to be more influential than the inclinations of the parties.

TABLE 7.2. ■ Party ideology and Amtrak subsidy

		Republican party ideology[a]			
		1–2		3–5	
Amtrak	Yes	12%	(3)	25%	(6)
subsidy	No	88	(21)	75	(18) (gamma = −.40)

		Democratic party ideology[b]			
		1–3		4–5	
Amtrak	Yes	19%	(6)	18%	(3)
subsidy	No	81	(25)	82	(14) (gamma = .06)

[a]McGregor (1978: 1020–1021); low scores indicate conservatism.

[b]McGregor (1978: 1022–1023); low scores indicate liberalism.

Although states have been involved with the railroads since the 1800s, subsidizing Amtrak is a fairly new activity. As noted earlier, the states vary considerably in the speed with which they adopt new policies. Some states may not subsidize Amtrak yet simply because it is a relatively new program and they are slow to adopt new programs. States with greater experience in developing and implementing new policies may provide a more hospitable environment for other policy initiatives.

As Table 7.3 indicates, the states that subsidize Amtrak tend to be the relatively innovative states. Using two different measures of innovativeness — one based on the speed with which states adopted a large number of innovations over several decades (the Walker Innovation Score), the other based on the speed with which states adopted innovations during the middle and latter parts of the twentieth century (the Savage Index) — consistent findings result: States that are slow to do new things are unlikely to subsidize passenger rail service. The tendencies are approximately of the same magnitude for both innovation measures.

TABLE 7.3. ■ Innovativeness and Amtrak subsidy

		Walker innovation score[a]				
		.395 or higher		.394 or lower		
Amtrak	Yes	26%	(8)	6%	(1)	
subsidy	No	74	(23)	94	(16)	(gamma = .70)

		Savage innovation ranking (later 20th century)[b]				
		Top 28		Bottom 20		
Amtrak	Yes	29%	(8)	5%	(1)	
subsidy	No	71	(20)	95	(19)	(gamma = .77)

[a]Walker (1971: 358); high scores indicate that a state is quick to adopt new programs.

[b]Savage (1978: 246–247); top-ranked states are quick to adopt new programs.

As long recognized, transportation policies have significant environmental consequences. Rail transportation can move a given number of passengers in a smaller expanse of land than automobiles can.[26] Trains consume less fuel per passenger mile than airplanes or, apparently, automobiles.[27] Greater fuel economy also results in less pollution.[28] In this view, subsidization of Amtrak may reflect a broader commitment to environmental protection. When confronting a new issue, public officials may seek to resolve it by the use of analogies to other situations for which decision rules have already been established.[29] The environmental implications of transportation decisions make the linkage between established environmental orientations and Amtrak subsidies a plausible one.

The evidence presented in Table 7.4 is consistent with this possibil-

TABLE 7.4. ■ Environmental concern and Amtrak subsidy

		Degree of environmental concern[a]				
		High		Low		
Amtrak	Yes	33%	(7)	7%	(2)	
subsidy	No	67	(14)	93	(25)	(gamma = .72)

[a]High environmental-concern states are those ranked in the top fifteen in air or water quality-control expenditures, 1970–71; see Jones (1976: 410–411).

ity. States with a previous history of significant efforts to combat air and water pollution are almost five times as likely to subsidize Amtrak service as states that have no history of major environmental protection efforts. The pattern is far from perfect, but the overall tendency is clear.

Although ideological factors, previous experience with policy innovations, and a previous record of environmental protection efforts are associated with decisions regarding Amtrak subsidies, the availability of slack resources may also shape adoption of those subsidies. Slack resources may be particularly critical for innovations with direct financial implications; adopting a subsidy program carries a tangible price tag. Resources may be less important for relatively symbolic innovations, which may have no impact on the state treasury.

The relationship between per capita income and subsidy decisions is consistent with the slack-innovation hypothesis (see Table 7.5). Comparatively affluent states are more than four times as likely to subsidize Amtrak service as the less affluent states. Only one of the seventeen poorest states supports passenger service.

TABLE 7.5. ■ Affluence and Amtrak subsidy

		Per capita income, 1982[a]			
		$10,100 or more		Less than $10,100	
Amtrak	Yes	26%	(8)	6%	(1)
subsidy	No	74	(23)	94	(16) (gamma = .70)

[a]*World Almanac* (1983: 116).

Two other state characteristics that cast light on the resource environment also capture, at least in part, aspects of the problem environment. Reality does not always fit into tidy analytical categories, but fully exploring the evidence may be more important than conceptual tidiness.

One of the conceptually ambiguous state characteristics is population. Since operating a passenger train carries certain minimum fixed costs—one or more locomotives, a crew, other rolling stock, roadbed in the Northeast Corridor, stations, and so forth—service will be more economical if there are larger numbers of customers. A state with few residents is unlikely to generate a high level of traffic volume. A state with several million residents can generate a substantial number of riders even if only a small fraction of the population travels by train. Passenger rail service is therefore likely to be more suitable in more populous states.

In a related vein, a more populous state can distribute those fixed costs over a larger number of taxpayers and therefore minimize the trauma associated with supporting at least a minimal level of operations. Moreover, as Olson argues, when contributions are voluntary (a state may choose whether to subsidize), those participants with a large stake may be more inclined to contribute.[30] A state with many residents is likely to have more people who cannot or prefer not to fly or drive. It will probably have more firms whose owners and managers are concerned about outside customers being able to reach those firms. A greater population may therefore enhance the likelihood of subsidizing Amtrak service.

This reasoning is strongly confirmed by the data in Table 7.6. A slim majority of the fifteen states with the largest populations subsidizes Amtrak, but only one of the thirty-three least populous states does. Moreover, not one of the twenty-five smallest states subsidizes. The size factor appears to be a significant influence on subsidy decisions.

TABLE 7.6. ■ Population, tourism, and Amtrak subsidies

		State population rank[a]				
		1–15		16–50		
Amtrak	Yes	53%	(8)	3%	(1)	
subsidy	No	47	(7)	97	(32)	(gamma = .95)

		Tourism spending, 1982[b]				
		$3 billion or more		Less than $3 billion		
Amtrak	Yes	42%	(8)	3%	(1)	
subsidy	No	58	(11)	97	(28)	(gamma = .91)

[a]*World Almanac* (1983: 607–631).
[b]*World Almanac* (1983: 607–631).

A second, conceptually ambiguous state characteristic is the size of the state's tourism industry. While a substantial portion of Amtrak's customers are business travelers, at least on some corridors, many are traveling for recreational purposes.[31] Since as many as 25 million people prefer not to fly[32] and others dislike driving or are unable to drive, train travel may be an important element of the tourist transportation system. States with particularly large tourism industries may have a particularly strong incentive to subsidize Amtrak. In this respect, tourism represents a portion of the problem environment.

In some respects, however, the size of the tourism industry may also reflect the availability of slack resources. If the subsidized service is successful in attracting tourist traffic, ticket purchases and other spending will help to cover the cost of the program.

As Table 7.6 indicates, tourism spending and subsidy decisions appear to be related. Just over two-fifths of the top nineteen states in spending by tourists subsidize Amtrak, but only one of the bottom twenty-nine does. In addition to promoting visits from people who cannot or prefer not to fly or drive, rail service may be a form of insurance against future fuel shortages for a state's tourist industry as well as a safeguard against the loss of service by other transportation modes.

Other aspects of the problem environment may shape state decisions regarding Amtrak subsidies, just as many other policy innovations are a reaction to a crisis or perceived policy problem. Most authorities believe that railroads have relatively high fixed costs. In that case, unit costs will be lower with higher traffic volume,[33] a situation most likely to be found in states with relatively concentrated populations. The broadly dispersed population of a rural state is likely to produce little traffic on any single corridor and therefore to generate high costs per traveler. This suggests that subsidies will be most productive in states with metropolitan populations. To the degree that state officials seek to allocate resources in productive ways, more metropolitan states should be more likely to subsidize Amtrak service.

In a related vein, rural states tend to be more oriented to highway building and to spend more on highways.[34] The legacy of past struggles to link rural areas to other parts of the state with all-weather roads and the continuing cost of those roads may mean that fewer dollars and less time and energy are available for other transportation programs in rural states. Policy issues compete for attention and resources, at least in some cases.[35]

Analysis supports the view that more metropolitan states should be more inclined to subsidize Amtrak service (see Table 7.7). The more metropolitan states are nearly nine times as likely to support passenger rail service as the less metropolitan states. Only one of the twenty-five least metropolitan states subsidizes Amtrak.

TABLE 7.7. ■ The problem environment and Amtrak subsidies

		Percent metropolitan, 1978[a]			
		64% or more		Less than 64%	
Amtrak	Yes	35%	(8)	4%	(1)
subsidy	No	65	(15)	96	(24) (gamma = .86)
		State area rank[b]			
		1–33		34–50	
Amtrak	Yes	28%	(9)	0%	(0)
subsidy	No	72	(23)	100	(16) (gamma = 1.0)

[a]*Statistical Abstract* (1980: 20).
[b]*World Almanac* (1983: 434).

One other aspect of the problem environment that may be relevant for transportation decisions is land area. In a state that is geographically large, the problems posed by covering great distances may enhance the salience of transportation issues generally. Moreover, Amtrak was originally created to be an intercity transportation system, not a commuter system, although legislation adopted in 1981 gave Amtrak some responsibilities in commuter service.[36] Overall, larger states may be more inclined to adopt subsidies to overcome the barriers created by distance.

This expectation too is supported by the evidence (see Table 7.7). Not one of the sixteen states with the smallest areas subsidizes Amtrak, but more than one fourth of the geographically large states do. Physical distances may enhance the value of long-distance transportation capabilities.

Multivariate Analysis

Multivariate analysis is difficult when relatively few cases display a phenomenon of interest. However, a decision flow model[37] is able to account for decisions regarding Amtrak subsidies with a high degree of accuracy (see Table 7.8). This model enables us to examine the combined effects of several variables. It is statistically similar in this application to an interactive model of the form

$$y = f(x_1) (x_2) + e$$

but with an important difference: The decisional flow model allows us to assign causal priority to the predictor variables and thus gain a sense of their relative contributions.

The first step of the model indicates that approximately two thirds of the states do not subsidize Amtrak because on one hand, their populations are too small to generate sufficiently high traffic volume to justify the cost of subsidies or on the other, to distribute the costs and provide a politically significant pool of beneficiaries. The greater stake of the more heavily populated states evidently encourages them to act.

The second step of the model reveals that of the most-populated states, the geographically large ones will tend to subsidize Amtrak but the smaller ones will not. In the latter group, the short distances involved are likely to make transportation problems appear less pressing and therefore to reduce support for subsidization. None of the other variables examined here could improve the fit of the model.

TABLE 7.8. ■ State decisions to subsidize Amtrak

Step number	Premise		Result	Accuracy	Cumulative percentage[a]
1	Was population at least 4.9 million?	No →	Do not subsidize (N = 33)	97%	67%
	↓ Yes				
2	Was area at least 44,000 square miles?	No →	Do not subsidize (N = 5)	100	77
	Yes				
		→	Subsidize (N = 10)	80	94

NOTE: The format of this table is adapted from Kingdon (1981: 244, 330).
[a]Percentage of cases correctly classified by this step and preceding steps.

The model achieves a high degree of predictive power, with forty-five of the forty-eight continental states behaving as predicted. Moreover, the two states that the model incorrectly predicts will subsidize Amtrak (Georgia and Texas) have both witnessed recent discussions of developing high-speed intercity passenger service.

Conclusions

While more than fifteen years have passed since the Arab oil embargo, the United States continues to rely heavily on passenger transportation modes that cannot function without enormous quantities of petroleum. With currently available technology, trains can move large numbers of people without petroleum if tracks are electrified, as some are in the Northeast, and the electricity is not generated by oil-fired plants.[38] Even without electrified tracks, the fuel efficiency of passenger trains with substantial loads is relatively high.

Given the limited ability of the national government to make the fundamental policy decisions needed to reorient the nation's passenger transportation system away from petroleum-intensive modes, the states have an opportunity to play a major role in shaping the nation's transportation policies. Moreover, state officials cannot be certain that national transportation decisions will always reflect the needs of individual states. In any case, an active state role may well be necessary.

At a more general level, whether rail passenger service should be subsidized at all remains controversial. Some observers prefer an end to subsidies and a shift to market allocation. In this view, subsidies simply create distortions in the transportation system and preserve a travel mode that does not meet consumer needs.[39]

Given the presence of substantial externalities in individual transportation decisions, however, private decisions cannot be depended upon to be fully efficient. The vulnerability of the national economy to interruptions in petroleum imports, the resulting vulnerability of the nation's foreign policy to influence by petroleum-exporting countries, and the capacity of the nation's domestic transportation system to function if available petroleum fuels are needed for military purposes in a prolonged international crisis are all affected by the sum of individual transportation decisions. The cost of deaths and injuries caused by automobiles is partly shifted to others through private and public mechanisms for socialization of risk. The conversion of croplands into roads has implications for everyone concerned about the world's food supply. To rely completely on market decisions is to encourage neglect of those considerations.

The adoption of Amtrak subsidies is concentrated in states with a combination of large population and large land area. Subsidy decisions, then, appear to be a response to the problem environment. However, to the degree that a large population makes raising funds easier, in the sense that the costs can be spread over more taxpayers, subsidies also reflect the availability of slack resources.

Those subsidies appear to be a comparatively fragile type of innovation; a number of the states that adopted Amtrak subsidies later terminated them.[40] An innovation that creates no new state agency and requires little or no state investment in fixed facilities may be particularly vulnerable to termination, at least in its early years. At the same time, a number of states have maintained their subsidy programs over an extended period and substantially improved the services available to their residents.[41]

NOTES

See Bibliography for full reference.

1. *Book of the States* (1986: 230–231).
2. Dye (1980).
3. Black and Runke (1975: 54); Sampson, Farris and Schrock (1985: 32, 544).

4. Grant and Nixon (1975: 478); Stover (1961: chapter 5).

5. *Railroad Facts* (1984: 32).

6. Chelf (1981: 172); Morris and Morris (1977: 14).

7. Bradley (1985: 40, 46).

8. Harper (1982: 382); Sampson, Farris, and Schrock (1985: 44–51).

9. Allen and Vellenga (1983: 17); Maze, Cook, and Carter (1984: 17).

10. *Amtrak National Train Timetables* (1985).

11. Locklin (1972: 855).

12. Harper (1982: 375); Locklin (1972: 859–860); Mulvey (1979).

13. Warren (1982: 157)

14. Gardiner (1978).

15. Warren (1982).

16. Cochran, Mayer, Carr, and Cayer (1982: 79).

17. Warren (1982: 145).

18. *World Almanac* (1983: 133).

19. Alston (1984); Craven (1977); *Railway Age* (1986).

20. Morris and Morris (1977: 198–199).

21. Hilton (1980: 53–54); Morris and Morris (1977: 199).

22. Hapgood (1976).

23. Colcord (1979: 3).

24. Colcord (1979: 14); Simon, Smithburg, and Thompson (1950: 27–30).

25. Hilton (1980: 53–54); Morris and Morris (1977: 199).

26. Dye (1981: 431); Morris and Morris (1977: 198–199).

27. See Harper (1982: 239), Hilton (1980: 52–53), *National Transportation Statistics* (1980: 106–113).

28. Harper (1982: 239); Morris and Morris (1977: 198).

29. See Cowart (1969), Fleishmann and Nice (1988), Hofferbert and Urice (1985), Walker (1969: 889). Note that this perspective suggests that innovativeness will be issue-specific: reactions to a proposal will depend on which decision rules are relevant to it.

30. Olson (1965: 27–36).

31. Hilton (1980: 37–39).

32. Bradley (1985: 49).

33. Harper (1982: 222).

34. Dye (1966: 157–161); Dye (1981: 431).

35. Cobb and Elder (1972: 45); Crenson (1971: 159–165).

36. Harper (1982: 385–386); Sampson, Farris, and Schrock (1985: 443).

37. See Kingdon (1981: 244, 330) and Nice (1983c: 594) for previous uses of decision flow models.

38. Alston (1984); Craven (1977).

39. See Hilton (1980) for a statement of this view.

40. Nice (1988a).

41. For a discussion of state-subsidized service between Los Angeles and San Diego, see Schiermeyer and Lange (1988).

8

Property Tax Relief

Introduction

The property tax consistently ranks as one of the most-disliked taxes in the United States. In ten public opinion surveys conducted between 1972 and 1982, the property tax was one of the two most frequently mentioned responses to the question "Which do you think is the worst tax—that is, the least fair?"[1] The popular dislike of the property tax has led to demands for property tax relief, the most sophisticated of which is state financed. The analysis that follows will seek to explain adoption of broad need-based programs of state-financed property tax relief to individuals.

The unpopularity of the property tax stems from a number of factors, one of which is that unlike sales or income taxes, it must be paid in one or two large painful chunks in many jurisdictions.[2] Taxpayers are therefore strongly reminded of how much they must pay each year. Sales taxes are paid a bit at a time, and many taxpayers are not certain how much they pay in sales taxes over the course of a year.

The eccentricities of the real estate market also contribute to the unpopularity of the property tax. During periods of rising real estate prices, property values may rise much faster than incomes. Unless local officials monitor the situation closely and revise tax rates downward, property taxes may rise more rapidly than taxpayers' incomes.[3] The administration of the property tax has further added to its unpopularity in some areas. Studies have found homes with similar market values being assessed at quite different values in the same city or county. Land with buildings has occasionally been assessed as a vacant lot because of failure to update records, and there are accounts of property that was entirely missing from the tax rolls.[4] Even efforts to improve the administration of the tax may cause complaints. A homeowner whose property has been underassessed for many years is likely to regard the correction of that situation as a tax increase.

Another element of the unpopularity of the residential property tax, at least in the minds of the public and many officials, is its alleged regressivity.[5] The actual burden of the property tax is a matter of considerable controversy in the literature. The case for regressivity is based on a number of elements. First, poorer families tend to devote a higher proportion of their incomes to housing costs, and the property tax reflects housing consumption, particularly if property taxes on rental housing are shifted to renters. In addition, assessment practices sometimes foster regressivity; more valuable property tends to be underassessed in some localities, producing lower effective rates for those properties than for less valuable ones. Finally, the property tax does not decline with declines in family income, as when a family's breadwinner retires or becomes unemployed, unless the family relocates to a less expensive residence.[6]

Critics of the regressivity view contend that analyses supporting it are typically based on current income. Analysis based on permanent income, on the other hand, indicates a proportional or even progressive tax burden. The property tax does not adjust for short-run income fluctuations, but in the long run wealthier people tend to have more expensive homes and consequently to pay more in property taxes. The typical property tax system does not have the maze of exemptions and deductions that have often permitted some upper-income individuals to avoid paying income taxes. Moreover, to the degree that the property tax is borne by capital and therefore property owners, the burden will be relatively progressive because property ownership is disproportionately concentrated in upper-income groups.[7] The degree to which property taxes are actually borne by capital appears uncertain,[8] but the newer view indicates that the property tax may not be as regressive as once thought.

Critics of property taxes have called for various reforms. One of the most important is state-financed relief to individuals. Approximately two thirds of the states currently have some form of state-financed relief, the vast majority "circuit breakers."[9] Proponents of relief programs have marshaled a number of arguments on their behalf.[10]

First, state-financed property tax relief can be a form of income redistribution to less affluent individuals, particularly if relief takes the form of a circuit breaker.[11] While circuit breakers vary from state to state, they typically involve several components. Initially, the state defines a "reasonable" tax for a taxpayer with a given income. Then tax-payers compare what they actually paid in property taxes to the state-defined reasonable amount. If a taxpayer paid more than that amount, he or she is eligible for a partial refund of the excess. That refund is paid from the state treasury.

The redistribution argument often assumes that the property tax is regressive,[12] although relief may be needed even if the tax is proportional or progressive, just as a proportional or progressive income tax typically includes some form of personal exemption or deduction.[13] Because renters are typically poorer than homeowners,[14] the redistributive effect will be considerably more pronounced if renters are included in the program. In addition, the redistributive effect will be greater if eligibility is general rather than restricted to particular groups such as the elderly. The need for redistribution, as well as preferences regarding distribution,[15] can be expected to vary from state to state.

State-financed relief can also be a form of indirect aid to local governments.[16] Because the relief programs typically involve state reimbursement for a share of the property taxes above some proportion of the taxpayer's income, those programs in effect channel state revenues into localities with high property taxes relative to local incomes. The state role can overcome the problems of localities with a high need for tax relief and little ability to finance it locally. That problem arises when poorer localities levy higher taxes to provide services at least roughly equivalent to those in wealthier jurisdictions.[17] Of course, inclinations to support local government activism to attack local problems and the ability to finance it may vary among states.

State-financed relief can help to reduce opposition to local revenue raising.[18] Although the property tax is disliked for many reasons, as noted earlier, the single most frequent criticism of it is its burden on the poor.[19] To the extent that relief programs reduce that burden, they may reduce opposition to local property taxes. This effect is in marked contrast to state-adopted tax ceilings, which substantially restrict local revenue raising. Once again, not all states may be equally supportive of local government activism.

A final point made by proponents of state-financed relief is more normative than financial: If a state adopts a program of relief, it should pay for it.[20] In this view, if state officials want to enjoy the political benefits of adopting relief, they should also assume the unpleasant task of financing that relief.

Scope

The coverage of state-financed relief programs varies greatly from state to state. At one extreme, sixteen states had no state-funded program in 1982.[21] In effect, no one was eligible for state-financed relief, regardless of need.

Of the states that have adopted some form of relief, a substantial number restrict eligibility to homeowners. Renters, who tend to be less affluent than homeowners,[22] receive no relief in those states, a situation that significantly limits the redistributive effect of those programs. Moreover, programs that exclude renters are less able to provide indirect aid to localities where renters are numerous and less able to reduce resistance to local revenue raising in those localities.

In addition to the distinction between programs that include renters and those that do not, relief programs that cover at least some renters differ in whether coverage is general (except for income limits) or restricted to certain groups, such as the elderly, the disabled, or veterans. General coverage is more capable of redistributing income to poorer people, for in the selective-coverage states a poor person who is not in one of the covered categories receives no help. In addition, broader coverage can provide indirect aid to localities with large numbers of poor people, whether they are young or old, disabled or not. A program of general coverage may also be more effective at reducing opposition to local revenue raising, for people in need of relief will receive it regardless of their special status.

Each state was scored according to whether it had any form of state-financed relief (1 point), whether at least some renters were eligible (1 point), and whether coverage extended to all homeowners and renters meeting economic criteria—that is, coverage not limited to elderly residents or the disabled (1 point). Summing the three items produces a cumulative scale (coefficient of reproduceability = 100 percent). High scores indicate broad relief coverage based on need; intermediate scores indicate selective coverage. A zero score indicates the absence of state-financed relief to individuals (see Table 8.1).

Influences

A number of factors may affect the coverage of state-financed relief to individuals. The literature indicates that relief programs are a method of providing benefits to poor people, redistributing funds to poorer lo-

TABLE 8.1. ■ State-financed property tax relief programs

Score	All homeowners and renters meeting economic criteria are covered	At least some renters are covered	State has some form of state-financed relief	
3	X	X	X	MD, MI, MN, NY, OR, VT, WI
2		X	X	AZ, CA, CO, CT, IL, IN, IA, KS, ME, MO, NV, NM, PA, RI, UT, WV
1			X	AL, AR, DL, ID, MA, ND, OH, OK, SD, WA, WY
0				AK, FL, GA, HA, KY, LA, MI, MT, NB, NH, NJ, NC, SC, TN, TX, VA

NOTE: *Book of the States* (1982: 400–401); coefficient of reproduceability = 100%.

calities, and reducing resistance to local revenue raising. Consequently, support for redistributing income, inclinations toward local government activism, the ability to finance relief, and the need for redistributing income from wealthier to poorer individuals may shape state responses to this innovation.

In general, liberals tend to be more supportive of government activism and redistributing income, and conservatives oppose government activism and redistribution. As a result, liberalism should encourage adoption of broadly based relief programs emphasizing need as a basis for receiving relief. The compatibility of an innovation and the ideological environment, in this view, will shape state decisions.

Two aspects of liberalism merit consideration. First, the ideologies of a state's political parties may influence the emphasis on need. Given the complexity of tax policies, both the policies themselves and their relationship to other elements of the budget process, organized support may be very important in shaping state decisions. Without some form of organization, a point of view may be dissipated by the complexities of tax policy-making and consequently have little impact. Party ideologies may therefore play a major role in shaping state decisions.[23]

A second aspect of liberalism involves the state electorate. To the degree that public policies reflect the views of active citizens, states with more liberal electorates should have greater emphasis on need in allocating tax relief. The comparatively high visibility of the property tax may cause state officials to be particularly sensitive to public sentiments. To do otherwise on an issue that arouses strong feelings in many people is to risk political defeat.

Three measures of electoral ideology will be used in this analysis. First, the percentage of the two-party vote for McGovern in the 1972 presidential election, which was more affected by issues and ideology but less affected by party loyalties than most other elections, indicates electoral liberalism.

In a similar vein, the percentage of the total vote for Reagan in 1980, another relatively ideological election (but more affected by party loyalties than the 1972 race),[24] provides evidence on electoral ideology. Finally, a recent analysis produced estimates of the ideological self-identification of state electorates by pooling surveys conducted between 1974 and 1982. Those estimates provide more direct evidence of electoral liberalism than does voting behavior, although the samples are rather small in some states.[25]

The breadth of relief coverage may also be influenced by state innovativeness. Where officials and citizens are accustomed to regular enactments of new policies and programs, a new idea such as providing state-financed tax relief may meet with a more cordial reception than where change is a rarity. That may be particuarly true for an innovation of this type, which will be very painful to terminate after it is in place.

The competitiveness of a state's political party system may also influence the adoption and coverage of property tax relief. According to Key, a one-party system has a bias toward inaction because it is often unable to mobilize organized support behind policy initiatives.[26] In addition, the weakness of parties in a one-party system is conducive to greater interest-group influence.[27] Because the interest-group system tends to overrepresent affluent groups[28] whose members will probably be in less need of tax relief, greater interest-group influence will probably mean less support for broad coverage. Finally, in a one-party system, votes are worth relatively little,[29] a situation that reduces the influence of lower-income groups because they have few other political resources.[30]

Overall, the literature suggests that program coverage should be narrower in states with less competitive parties; in that context there will be less pressure for innovation and less capacity for adopting innovations.

Two measures of party competition will be used in this analysis. Both are based on gubernatorial and legislative elections. Ranney's index covers the period from 1962 to 1973; a more recent version covers elections from 1974 to 1980.[31] Both measures will be used because previous research indicates that relationships among state traits can shift over time.[32]

While the interest-group system in general may not be particularly supportive of relief programs, one interest group has supported them — the elderly. Their support stems from the fact that property taxes do not decline as income falls at retirement.[33] The elderly represent a base of support for relief and are natural allies for nonelderly lower-income groups seeking similar relief.

The influence of the elderly can be measured in a number of ways. One indicator is the proportion of the state population over sixty-five. A state with proportionally more elderly residents will have proportionally more need for relief because of the income decline that usually occurs at retirement. A problem may result, however, if a large but unorganized elderly population has difficulty gaining attention for its needs. An alternative measure is the proportion of the state population belonging to the American Association for Retired Persons (AARP), a major interest group representing senior citizens. A potential problem with this approach is the general tendency for people who join groups to be more affluent than nonjoiners.[34] AARP members may therefore have less need for relief than elderly nonjoiners.

Although ideological, partisan, and interest-group forces may shape state decisions regarding property tax relief, the slack hypothesis holds that availability of resources to support a relief program may also be a major consideration. A state-financed relief program, particularly one with broad coverage, will generate immediate and continuing demands on the state treasury. Moreover, once the benefits begin to flow, they are likely to be very difficult to terminate. Officials in wealthier states are likely to have greater confidence in their ability to meet those financial demands. Officials in poorer states may be reluctant to make a long-term commitment to a program with potentially high and uncertain costs, for program costs will depend in part on the tax decisions of many local governments.

The supply of economic resources, however, may also be an indicator of the problem environment. Greater affluence will leave relatively few people who are unduly burdened by property taxation and therefore reduce the need for relief. In a similar fashion, a state with relatively few poor people and a uniform distribution of income will have less need for relief. A proportionally large poverty population and an uneven distribution of income, with some very wealthy people and some very poor people, will produce a greater need for relief. According to this perspective, and contrary to the slack-resources model, states that are less affluent and with larger poverty populations should be more likely to adopt state-financed relief.

The geographical distribution of a state's population may also influence adoption of relief. As a state's population is increasingly concentrated in urban and metropolitan areas, people are more likely to be affected by one another's actions. Problems grow less amenable to individual solutions, and government intervention becomes more necessary. Social problems may grow more visible, leading to a greater acceptance of government action. In addition, a close concentration of many different types of property may lead more people to feel, correctly or not, that some property owners are receiving preferential treatment. A local news story on an elderly couple being forced from their home by rising property taxes will reach more readers and viewers in a metropolitan area than in a rural setting. Overall, states with more urban and metropolitan populations may consequently be more likely to adopt relief programs with broad coverage.

Two other aspects of the problem environment for relief policies may be diversity and homeownership. In a diverse population, some people will receive benefits while others pay, a circumstance that may lead the latter group to demand tax relief.[35] Moreover, diversity makes assessment more difficult,[36] and the resulting problems may produce additional demand for relief. The impact of homeownership is more difficult to predict. Because homeowners receive explicit bills for their property taxes but renters' property taxes are concealed in their rents, the former group may be more sensitive to property taxes and more supportive of relief.[37] Conversely, because homeowners tend to be wealthier than renters, homeowners may have less need for relief and therefore reduce the coverage of relief programs.

Other aspects of the problem environment involve the tax system itself. Property taxes that consume a relatively large share of personal income and state-local own-source revenues that consume a large income share may come to be regarded as a crisis that demands a dramatic response—a crisis innovation. Certainly much of the rhetoric surrounding the "tax revolt" suggests a crisis or at least the perception of one, and Gold notes that states without circuit breakers generally have relatively low property taxes.[38]

Property taxes relative to state income and total state-local revenues relative to state income may be stimulants of relief programs. A state's citizens may demand one to provide relief from burdensome property taxes, or the program may be seen as a form of general tax relief from all types of state and local revenue burdens. In addition to the level of property taxation, changes in property taxes may stimulate demands for relief.[39] An individual facing a tax increase may be more impressed by the increase than by the knowledge that property taxes elsewhere are higher.

Analysis

The zero-order relationships indicate that broader coverage of state-financed property tax relief reflects state inclinations toward policy liberalism (see Table 8.2). Liberal ideologies in both parties are associated

TABLE 8.2. ■ **Zero-order relationships between state characteristics and state-financed property tax relief scale**

	Scale
Republican party ideology (McGregor, 1978)	.49[d]
Democratic party ideology (McGregor, 1978)	−.55[d]
Percent for McGovern, 1972	.49[d]
Percent for Reagan, 1980	−.17
Electoral conservatism (Wright, Erickson, and McIver, 1985)	−.39[b]
Innovation score (Walker, 1969)	.42[c]
Party competition, 1974–1980	.31[a]
Party competition, 1962–1973	.47[d]
Percent of population over 65, 1976	.10
Percent of population over 65, 1970	.18
AARP members per 1,000 population, 1978	.36[b]
Median income 1975	.16
Gini index of income inequality (Dye, 1969)	−.50[d]
Percent of population in poverty	−.44[d]
Percent metropolitan, 1978	.17
Percent urban, 1970	.23
Diversity (Sullivan, 1973)	.35[b]
Percentage of housing units owner-occupied, 1970	.12
State and local property tax effort, 1969–1970[d]	.35[b]
State and local own-source revenue effort, 1969–1970	−.12
State and local property tax effort, 1977	.10
State and local own-source revenue effort, 1977	.13
1977 state and local property tax effort divided by 1967–1970 property tax effort	−.17

[a]$P < .02$
[b]$P < .01$
[c]$P < .002$
[d]$P < .001$

[e]*Book of the States* (1982–83: 400–401); states with a score of zero have no state-financed property tax relief for individuals. A score of 1 indicates some state programs, however limited. A score of 2 indicates that at least some renters are eligible for relief. A score of 3 indicates that all homeowners and renters meeting economic criteria are eligible for relief without having to meet other noneconomic criteria such as age or disability.

with adoption of broader, need-based relief programs (the negative sign for Democratic party ideology occurs because low values for that measure denote liberalism). In addition, states with more liberal electorates, as measured by the McGovern vote and the Wright, Erikson, and McIver measure, place greater emphasis on need, as do innovative states.

States with more competitive political parties and proportionally more AARP members tend to emphasize need more in relief programs. Contrary to expectations, states with relatively unequal income distributions and proportionally larger poverty populations place less emphasis on need in relief policies. Greater population diversity is associated with broader, need-based coverage, as expected. Finally, emphasis on need is greater in states with higher property tax effort, 1969–1970. The other state traits display no zero-order relationships with relief provisions.

Stepwise multiple regression analysis of the coverage of state programs confirms the importance of ideological factors in shaping the provisions (see Table 8.3).[40] Democratic liberalism and Republican liberalism are both associated with broader relief coverage. The presence of both party ideology measures in the model indicates that each party exerts an independent influence on relief decisions; the two ideology measures are only moderately associated ($r = -.45$). Unexpectedly, property tax effort is negatively related to breadth of coverage. Finally, more urbanized states tend to have broader coverage.

TABLE 8.3. ■ Stepwise regression analysis of property tax relief provisions

Predictor	b	beta	F	R^2
		N = 48[a]		
Democratic party ideology	−.52	−.67	18.17[b]	.48
Republican party ideology	.26	.36	7.91[c]	
State-local property tax effort, 1977	−.03	−.44	7.14[d]	
Percent urban, 1970	.02	.24	4.17[d]	

[a]Alaska and Hawaii omitted because of missing data. All of the predictors in Table 1 were entered in the stepwise analysis, but only the four above emerged as significant.
[b]$p < .001$
[c]$p < .01$
[d]$p < .05$

The multivariate analysis supports the contention that state-financed programs, particularly broad ones emphasizing need, result from ideological forces. State-funded programs can increase the progressivity (or reduce the regressivity) of local government finance, reduce resistance to local revenue raising, and provide indirect aid to poorer localities. All these results are consistent with liberal ideologies.

In a similar fashion, the relationship between urbanization and program coverage is consistent with the argument that urban life, with its increasing interdependence and impersonality, leads to greater need for government intervention and therefore stimulates innovation. The result is that more urbanized states adopt state-financed relief and provide broader coverage.

The unexpected finding that emerges from the multivariate analysis is the negative relationship between property tax effort and program coverage. Two forces may be at work. First, the cost of a relief program will be higher, other things being equal, as property taxes relative to income rise and the coverage of the program grows more general.[41] When ideological factors are held constant, the rising cost of relief when property taxes relative to income grow higher may lead to narrower coverage of relief programs. Second, a specific aversion to property taxation may be significant. If public opinion is particularly hostile to property taxes, we would expect to find both low property tax effort and broad programs to relieve excess property tax burdens when other factors are held constant.

Conclusions

The property tax, like the weather, is something almost everyone seems to complain about. Unlike the weather, however, dissatisfaction with the property tax has led people to do something about it. State officials faced with complaints about property taxation must decide whether the state should finance relief. Moreover, if they decide to provide relief, they must decide whether to make it available to all who need relief or to restrict coverage to certain groups. At the most restrictive extreme, no one receives relief, regardless of need. At intermediate levels, relief is available to some groups, but others with equivalent need are excluded based on other criteria, such as age or whether they rent or own their residence. At the least restrictive extreme, determination of relief is entirely need-based; advanced age, homeownership, or other qualifications are not needed.

The breadth of coverage in relief programs, as measured here, may consequently be viewed as the relative emphasis on need as a basis for providing relief. That interpretation is consistent with the bulk of the multivariate analysis. Liberal party ideologies and urbanization, as stimulants of government action to meet social needs, are associated with a more need-based response to relief.

On a broader level, this analysis indicates that political forces, notably ideological ones, at least occasionally have a significant policy impact. Although the importance of socioeconomic factors for many policy decisions has been firmly established, this analysis indicates that political factors do have policy influence, at least occasionally. That may be particularly true for issues that arouse strong feelings, such as property tax relief, and are unclearly defined. In the case of the property tax, its unpopularity is clear, but experts differ on the distribution of its burden. In that context, ideological forces, which can help to clarify uncertain situations, serve as guideposts to officials in making specific decisions.

NOTES

See Bibliography for full reference.

1. Advisory Commission on Intergovernmental Relations (1982: 38–41).

2. Musgrave and Musgrave (1980: 488).

3. Musgrave and Musgrave (1980: 488).

4. See Lowery (1982); Maxwell and Aronson (1977: 145–155).

5. Advisory Commission on Intergovernmental Relations (1982: 43); Musgrave and Musgrave (1980: 485).

6. Henry (1984: 355); Maxwell and Aronson (1977: 138–139); Mikesell (1982: 225); Musgrave and Musgrave (1980: 481–487); Netzer (1966: 5, 49–59); Paul (1975: 22–23); Peterson, Solomon, Madjid, and Apgar (1973: 119).

7. See Aaron (1975); Maxwell and Aronson (1977: 139–140); Musgrave and Musgrave (1980: 481–487); Netzer (1966: 57–58).

8. Maxwell and Aronson (1977: 140).

9. *Book of the States* (1982: 400–401).

10. Not all the authors cited in this section are proponents of state-financed property tax relief, but the literature discusses the arguments made on behalf of relief.

11. Aaron (1975: 75).

12. Aaron (1975: 74).

13. Advisory Commission on Intergovernmental Relations (1975: 14–16).

14. Mikesell (1982: 225).

15. Bear in mind that objective measures of need, such as property tax levels, the extent of poverty, and perceptions of need, as well as inclinations to respond to needs, are not necessarily the same. People in jurisdictions with similar needs may have very different perceptions of the needs. See Dye (1984: 103–109).

16. Aaron (1975: 74–75); Gold (1979: 315–316); Peterson (1976: 102).

17. See Advisory Commission on Intergovernmental Relations (1975: 8).

18. Mikesell (1982: 225); Peterson (1976: 102).

19. Advisory Commission on Intergovernmental Relations (1982: 42).

20. Advisory Commission on Intergovernmental Relations (1975: 8); Gold (1979: 315–316).

21. *Book of the States* (1982: 400–401).

22. Mikesell (1982: 225).

23. For other evidence on party ideologies and tax policy, see Nice (1982).

24. See Hill and Luttbeg (1983: 50).

25. Wright, Erikson, and McIver (1985).

26. Key (1949: 303–310).

27. Schattschneider (1942: 196).

28. Schattschneider (1960: 31–33); Schlozman (1984).

29. Schattschneider (1960: 80).
30. See also Burnham (1970: 133); Sorauf (1984: 429–430).
31. Ranney (1976: 61); Bibby, Cotter, Gibson, and Huckshorn (1983: 66).
32. Dye (1984: 300–302).
33. Henry (1984: 355); Mikesell (1982: 225).
34. See Verba and Nie (1972: 203).
35. Stein (1984: 42).
36. Lowery (1982, 1984).
37. Stein, Hamm, and Freeman (1983: 189–190).
38. Gold (1979: 56).
39. See Stein, Hamm, and Freeman (1983); Stein (1984).
40. The property tax relief scale may be closer to an ordinal measure than interval level, the latter being assumed for regression analysis significance tests. However, multiple regression is not particularly sensitive to violations of the assumptions regarding the dependent variable (see Bohrnstedt and Knoke [1982: 231], Kerlinger and Pedhazur [1973: 47–48], and the studies they cite). Following Blalock (1979: 54), the predictors that emerged from the multivariate analysis in Table 8.2 were used to predict each item in the property tax scale using discriminant analysis. The results were generally consistent with the regression results in Table 8.2, although urbanization was essentially unrelated to whether a state had general coverage of homeowners and renters rather than limited or no coverage.
41. On the latter point, see Advisory Commission on Intergovernmental Relations (1975: 6).

Deregulation of Intimate Behavior

Introduction

Policy innovations are frequently regarded as the creation of new programs and new agencies. The implication of that perspective is that innovative government is expanding government – more services, more agencies, and often higher costs. While that impression is sometimes accurate, the distinctive charactertistic of an innovation is the quality of being new, at least in the context of the organization adopting it. A policy change that involves the elimination of a long-established policy or program may therefore be properly regarded as an innovation.

Controversies regarding whether government should control, regulate, or otherwise seek to influence various activities are at the heart of many political issues.[1] Those controversies do not end when a new program is adopted. Indeed, they may intensify. Terminating or cutting back agencies and programs is typically difficult in most cases. Programs provide benefits that once available, are not easily ended. Agencies provide employment and status, neither easily terminated. The sheer difficulty of passing legislation means that once a policy is in place, it will be difficult to repeal.[2]

In spite of these difficulties, however, agencies and programs are sometimes pared back and are occasionally eliminated altogether.[3] In recent years the extent of government regulation over a number of activities has significantly declined. The following analysis will seek to explore state deregulation of sodomy.

A major component of the deregulation effort has been in the economic arena. Critics have charged that economic regulation often served

113

the interests of regulated industries more than consumers and that the costs of economic regulation often outweighed the benefits. A combination of national legislation and executive orders has produced substantial reductions in regulation of financial institutions, railroads, airlines, and trucking.[4] Not all the results of deregulation have been positive, as the experience of the savings and loan industry in the 1980s amply demonstrates. Nevertheless, deregulation of various parts of the economy is a striking example of innovation that yields less government rather than more.

A second major facet of deregulation in recent years affects intimate behavior. The states have a long tradition of involvement in the private lives of their citizens. State policies have regulated (with varying degrees of effectiveness) marriage, divorce, and adoption, and the states have a history of trying to regulate the sexual practices of their residents, including contraceptives and abortion.

Here too, regulatory efforts produced a substantial number of complaints. Critics have charged that public policies regarding contraceptives, abortion services, and sexual activities between consenting adults produced costs that outweighed their benefits. In the blunt words of one observer, "If it were not for the tragedy involved, one of the great farces of American history would be its laws designed to control and regulate sexual behavior."[5] According to the critics, those laws have led to governmental intrusion into private lives and have been enforced inconsistently, with some people being punished for activities that are tolerated when other people engage in them. Public policies regarding intimate behavior have sometimes provoked intense conflict, from the days when members of the American Birth Control League were assaulted and their meetings disrupted by opponents of birth-control programs[6] to the more recent wave of abortion clinic bombings.[7]

In contrast to economic deregulation, much of the deregulation of intimate behavior has come from the U.S. Supreme Court. In a series of decisions the Court struck down state laws banning the use or dispensing of contraceptives and laws that the Court concluded placed undue restrictions on access to abortion.[8] The Court based these decisions on the premises that the U.S. Constitution implies a right to privacy and that at least some aspects of intimate behavior are protected by that right. The Court's activities, particularly in the abortion field, have proved highly controversial.

A less visible aspect of the movement to deregulate intimate behavior has been the repeal of state laws that make sodomy between consenting adults a crime.[9] The movement to repeal those laws, practically universal at one time, has now succeeded in just over half the states.[10] The drive to deregulate sodomy has had a number of factors working in its favor.

First, laws seeking to regulate the sexual practices of consenting adults, including married couples, are extremely difficult to enforce. Without the ability to monitor private residences, police cannot detect many violations.[11] Second, available evidence indicates a lack of behavioral support for the laws; nongenital intercourse is commonly practiced by both heterosexuals and homosexuals.[12] Third, a recent Gallup Poll indicates that public opinion does not support state regulation of private, consensual adult sexual behavior, particularly between heterosexuals but also between homosexuals.[13] Finally, in an era when police resources are strained to the limit and beyond by violent crime, drug abuse, and other serious offenses, deregulation of less-serious offenses may help to target law-enforcement efforts where they are most needed.

In spite of these forces supporting decriminalization of sodomy, it remains a crime in twenty-four states, with maximum prison terms of up to twenty years (see Table 9.1). Moreover, state laws prohibiting sodomy have been upheld by the Supreme Court, in contrast to the Court's rulings on laws governing other intimate behaviors. The Court majority in *Bowers* v. *Hardwick* justified the different treatment of sodomy laws by contending that homosexual practices do not have the same standing in the nation's history and tradition as marriage, procreation, and the like. However, dissenting justices in the *Bowers* case noted that the law in that case applied to heterosexual couples as well as homosexuals. That law was later used to prosecute and convict a man for having oral sex with his wife.[14] Overall, then, the Supreme Court has given the states considerable latitude in prohibiting or permitting sodomy.

TABLE 9.1. ■ States that prohibit sodomy

Alabama	Mississippi
Arizona	Missouri
Arkansas	Montana
Florida	Nevada
Georgia	North Carolina
Idaho	Oklahoma
Kansas	Rhode Island
Kentucky	South Carolina
Louisiana	Tennessee
Maryland	Texas
Michigan	Utah
Minnesota	Virginia

SOURCE: Adapted from Press and colleagues (1986: 37).

The analysis that follows will seek to explain variations in state responses to the effort to legalize sodomy. The responses may cast light on the dynamics of innovation when it involves a contraction in governmental control of behavior that arouses considerable controversy.

Potential Influences on State Decisions

A prominent element of the controversy over deregulating intimate behavior is ideological. Conservatives who seek to maintain traditional values have often called for preserving and even extending government regulation of private behavior, including sexual practices between consenting adults.[15] These social conservatives,[16] in contrast to economic conservatives' preference for limited government, support the use of government power to maintain traditional values. In this view, conservatism should encourage continuation of laws prohibiting sodomy.

Conservatism may also encourage the survival of prohibitions against sodomy because of its general skepticism regarding change and reform. Current policies and programs may have deficiencies, but a new policy creates uncertainty and the risk of even greater deficiencies. If deregulation of sodomy is seen as a form of social experimentation, conservatives, who tend to be wary of such enterprises, should be less enthusiastic about repeal of prohibitions. The obvious risk of encouraging behavior that many social conservatives believe is sinful is likely to spur their opposition.

To the degree that ideological forces must be organized in order to exert significant influence in the policy-making process, the ideological leanings of state political parties may be particularly influential in shaping decisions. Party ideologies help to shape the choices presented to voters and the types of opposition public officials are likely to face. Conservative parties should therefore encourage preservation of laws against sodomy.

A second component of the ideological climate is political culture. The traditionalistic culture, with its emphasis on preserving the established order and suspicion of change, is likely to encourage preservation of sodomy laws. The moralistic culture, with its support for progress and reform, may encourage repeal of sodomy laws, although that prediction is less clear-cut. The relatively broad view of government powers and responsibilities in the moralistic culture may encourage continued government regulation of intimate behavior in some instances. The individualistic culture, which emphasizes private decision making over governmental direction by and large, should foster deregulation of sodomy laws to give individuals more freedom from public restrictions.[17]

The opinion climate of state policy-making can be assessed in other fashions. The 1972 presidential election, which was strongly influenced by issue concerns, provides a behavioral indication of the ideological leanings of state voters. In addition, survey estimates of the ideological leanings of state electorates provide a comparatively direct assessment of the opinion climate.[18] As the preceding discussion indicates, conservatism is likely to encourage continuation of prohibitions against sodomy.

One other component of the ideological-cultural environment is innovativeness. Where officials have considerable experience with new initiatives and the public is accustomed to program changes, a new policy such as deregulation of sodomy may be easier to adopt. Where officials and the public are more accustomed to preserving the status quo, continuation of antisodomy laws is more likely to occur.

State decisions regarding prohibition of sodomy may be affected by the socioeconomic environment, which infuences many policy decisions. Research indicates that more highly educated individuals are more likely to favor legalization of homosexuality and more likely to accept the practice of oral sex.[19] A more-educated population may therefore encourage deregulation of sodomy.

In a related vein, individuals with higher incomes are more likely to favor legalization of homosexuality.[20] As a result, more affluent states should be more likely to deregulate sodomy (most state sodomy laws apply to heterosexuals as well as homosexuals, however). Poorer states, by contrast, should be more likely to preserve legal prohibitions if the opinions of different income levels are influential in shaping state decisions.

Affluence may also influence decisions in a very different way. As noted earlier, officials in wealthier states typically find that raising revenues is considerably easier than in poorer states. Officials in poorer states may therefore be particularly anxious to find ways to reduce demands on their overburdened treasuries. Deregulation of sodomy may help to target scarce resources to more crucial law-enforcement needs, and that targeting will be most essential in poorer states. If that reasoning is correct, poorer states should be more likely to deregulate sodomy.[21]

A final component of the socioeconomic environment is urbanization, although the nature of its impact is difficult to predict. On one hand, greater urbanization, with its growing interdependence and weakening social controls, may lead to more acceptance of government activism to control behavior that some people regard as offensive, immoral, or even frightening. The wide variety of behaviors encountered in many urban settings may lead people to support public policies designed to regulate that behavior. In this view, greater urbanization and population density should encourage preservation of antisodomy laws.

An alternative possibility, however, is that life in urban areas may encourage greater tolerance of different lifestyles.[22] People may become accustomed to encountering a variety of behaviors and gradually grow less alarmed about many of those behaviors. If this perspective is correct, more densely populated states should be more likely to repeal sodomy laws. Rural and small-town environments may produce less tolerance and consequently more support for preserving laws against sodomy.

While policy innovations sometimes emerge as a response to the problem environment, assessing its role in this particular case is extremely difficult in view of two considerations. First, the nature and even existence of the problem is a matter of considerable dispute. Some regard sodomy as a mortal sin that must be eliminated, but others believe that healthy sexual expression can take a variety of forms.[23] Unlike starvation, airplane crashes, and a variety of other phenomena that are universally regarded as problems, then, sodomy is a problem for some people but not others. In addition, there is no dependable information on the extent of the practice in each state.

A partial solution to this difficulty, though far from a perfect one, is to focus on the definition or perception of the problem environment, for definition of problems and issues is a key phase of policy-making,[24] particularly when there are major differences of opinion whether something is a problem. If sodomy is perceived as a sin and an abomination, repeal of prohibition is likely to be difficult. Conversely, if sodomy is regarded as normal sexual behavior, governmental prohibitions will seem unnecessary.

Definitions of acceptable sexual behavior are a significant feature of many religions. The Reverend Jerry Falwell,[25] noting that the Bible condemns the practice of homosexuality, contends that the law should prohibit immoral practices, even between consenting adults. In a related vein, official Roman Catholic doctrine holds that the primary purpose of intercourse is procreation.[26] The Latter-day Saint (Mormon) faith also places considerable emphasis on procreation. The prominence of religions with relatively strict doctrines regarding sexual activity should in this view affect whether sodomy is defined as a sin. Where those religions dominate, the identification of sodomy as a problem is more likely to dominate. That should in turn encourage maintenance of laws prohibiting sodomy. From a doctrinal standpoint, these religions include Baptists, Catholics, and Latter-day Saints.

Of course, official doctrine and the views of church members do not necessarily coincide. American Catholics tend to have less traditional values regarding sex and family life than Protestants, official doctrines notwithstanding. In addition, Catholics are more likely to favor legalization of homosexuality than are Protestants.[27] The influence of religious groups, in light of this evidence, is best examined in terms of individual faiths.

Analysis

Preliminary analysis supports most of the initial hypotheses (see Table 9.2). Party ideology is substantially associated with policies regarding sodomy, particularly for the Democratic party, and both the relationships indicate that ideological conservatism in the state parties is associated with laws prohibiting sodomy. In a similar fashion, cultural traditionalism is associated with laws prohibiting sodomy, but moralism displays little relationship to the state policies at the zero-order level. States with conservative electorates, as indicated by a low vote for McGovern in 1972 or a high score on the Wright, Erikson, and McIver index of electoral conservatism, have tended to retain prohibitions against sodomy.

As expected, more innovative states are likely to have deregulated sodomy. Wealthier and more-educated states display the same tendency. However, population density and urbanization are essentially unrelated to policy decisions on this issue.

TABLE 9.2. ■ State characteristics and sodomy laws

	State law prohibits sodomy[a]
Republican ideology (McGregor, 1978)	−.34
Democratic ideology (McGregor, 1978)	.59
Traditionalism	.54
Moralism	−.18
Percent for McGovern, 1972	−.48
Electoral conservatism (Wright, Erickson, and McIver, 1985)	.44
Innovation (Walker, 1969)	−.44
Median education, 1960	−.40
Median income, 1959	−.48
Population density, 1960	−.16
Percent urban, 1960	−.11
Percent Catholic	−.40
Percent Baptist	.59
Percent Mormon	.18

[a]Existence of prohibition = 1; absence of prohibition = 0 (Press and colleagues, 1986: 37).

Contrary to official doctrine but consistent with public opinion research, states with larger Catholic populations are likely to have legalized sodomy. By contrast, states with relatively large Baptist memberships tend to retain laws against sodomy. The Latter-day Saint faith has relatively little influence at the zero-order level.

Because of the large number of independent variables and the substantial correlations among them, stepwise discriminant analysis[28] was used to develop a parsimonious model of state decisions regarding prohibition of sodomy (see Table 9.3). States prohibiting sodomy tend to have conservative Democratic parties. None of the other variables examined in this analysis could significantly improve the fit of the model, and the relationship between Democratic ideology and prohibition of sodomy survives controls for the other independent variables used one at a time and also survives the introduction of a dummy variable for the South. Overall, nearly three fourths of the states behave as the model predicts.[29]

TABLE 9.3. ■ Discriminant analysis of state sodomy laws

State law prohibits sodomy[a]	
Standardized canonical discriminant function coefficient	Canonical correlation = .59 Wilks's lambda = .66 % correctly classified = 72.92 Chi^2 = 19.124[b]
Democratic party ideology 1.00 (McGregor, 1978)	
Group centroids: Group 0 −.71 Group 1 .71	

[a]Existence of prohibition = 1; absence of prohibition = 0.
[b]$p < .0001$ with 1 d.f. N = 48.

Factor analysis of the independent variables indicates that Democractic ideology is part of an underlying dimension representing ideological-cultural orientations, as indicated by Democratic ideology, the Baptist population, and Elazar's culture measures. Viewed from that perspective, and in light of the zero-order relationships, the discriminant analysis indicates that prohibitions against sodomy reflect an underlying ideological-cultural conservatism. The innovation of repealing those laws is concentrated in the more liberal states. Where more conservative views predominate, prohibitions against sodomy are more likely to survive.

Summary and Conclusions

A common generalization regarding government agencies and programs holds that once they are created, they are nearly impossible to eliminate.[30] Although the durability of public agencies and programs is clear, the recent evidence on deregulation indicates that programs can be cut back or even eliminated outright, although not without difficulty. Substantial reductions in government regulations of economic activity and intimate behavior indicate that programs can be reduced or terminated.

While the Supreme Court has made major contributions to deregulating intimate behavior, the states have also played a significant role. Just over half the states have legalized sodomy between consenting adults, but the remaining states still outlaw the practice. Moreover, the Supreme Court has upheld the constitutionality of those prohibitions.

The results of this analysis indicate that legalization of sodomy can be explained largely in ideological-cultural terms. States that have deregulated sodomy tend to have more liberal Democratic parties. Democratic ideology in this case serves as a carrier for a broader, underlying ideological-cultural dimension, as reflected in Democratic ideology, the relative size of the Baptist population, and Elazar's culture measures. In states at the more conservative end of that dimension, unconventional sexual behavior is likely to have more opponents, and an innovation legalizing that behavior is consequently less likely to be adopted.

Although conservatives often denounce government activism and regulation, there is little doubt that conservatives will often support governmental intervention that promotes their values. This is an example of Schattschneider's scope of conflict: Views regarding the appropriate decision-making arena are closely linked to preferred outcomes.[31] If people believe a particular arena, whether public or private, national or state, will not produce the outcome they desire, they are likely to support action in a different arena. Conservatives may therefore be advocates of governmental activism when it is more likely to produce outcomes they desire than is private decision making. Conversely, liberals may at times defend private-sector autonomy when the alternative is a conservative governmental policy.

The comparatively modest influence of socioeconomic factors is hardly surprising in light of the limited direct fiscal consequences resulting from sodomy laws. In addition, the theoretical basis for expecting any relationship between socioeconomic characteristics and sodomy laws was largely based on attitudinal factors. When more direct attitudinal measures are incorporated into the analysis, the limited independent influence of socioeconomic traits naturally follows.

NOTES

See Bibliography for full reference.

1. Schattschneider (1960).
2. Kaufman (1976).
3. Levine (1980).
4. Meier (1985: 286–287); Sampson, Farris, and Shrock (1985: chapter 22).
5. McCary (1973: 457).
6. Gamson (1975: 85).
7. Nice (1988b).
8. For example, *Griswold* v. *Connecticut* 381 U.S. (1965) and *Roe* v. *Wade* 410 U.S. 113 (1973). Controversial Supreme Court rulings have sometimes faced compliance problems. See Abraham (1975: 337–339) and Goldman and Jahnige (1985: 221–224) and the studies they cite.
9. The legal definition of *sodomy* varies somewhat from state to state, but the definitions virtually all include oral and anal sex, and the vast majority of state laws cover heterosexual and homosexual acts. Those laws have been upheld by the U.S. Supreme Court (*Doe* v. *Commonwealth's Attorney,* 96 S. Ct. 1489 [1976], 543).
10. Press and colleagues (1986).
11. See McCary (1973: 459); Press and colleagues (1986: 36).
12. Kogan (1973: 89, 324); McCary (1973: 460); Moore (1969: 345– 370).
13. Press and colleagues (1986: 38).
14. See *Bowers* v. *Hardwick* 478 U.S. (1986) and the discussion in Feeley and Krislov (1990: 903–906).
15. Falwell (1984: 294, 298–299).
16. For discussions of social conservatives, see Asher (1984: 287–288); Erikson, Luttbeg, and Tedin (1980: 163–164); and Scammon and Wattenberg (1970).
17. See Elazar (1972: 96–102).
18. Wright, Erikson, and McIver (1985).
19. *Gallup Report* (1986a: 3); Kinsey, Pomercy, and Martin (1948: 368–371).
20. *Gallup Report* (1986a: 3).
21. Laws against consensual sodomy are not enforced with great frequency. As a result, actual cost savings from deregulation would probably be very small.
22. See Erikson, Luttbeg, and Tedin (1980: 183–185).
23. Kogan (1973: 324).
24. Bachrach and Baratz (1962).
25. Falwell (1984: 294, 299).
26. Heffernan (1984).
27. *Gallup Report* (1986a, 1986b).
28. For some cautionary comments regarding stepwise techniques, see Wonnacott and Wonnacott (1979: 407–410).
29. With Alaska and Hawaii omitted because of missing data, random assignment would correctly classify 50 percent of the states.
30. Kaufman (1976).
31. Schattschneider (1960).

State Ownership of Freight Railroads

Introduction

In an overview of the history of railroading in North America, Hollingsworth and Whitehouse titled the chapter on recent developments "Struggle in the Space Age."[1] In many respects, America's railroads are indeed in the midst of a serious struggle whose ultimate outcome is yet to be fully determined. Because the result has enormous implications for the nation's transportation system, economy, and national security, many observers have expressed concern over the plight of the railroads and have proposed a variety of solutions. The following analysis will seek to explain adoption of an innovative state program to preserve rail freight service—public ownership of railroads.

The most dramatic evidence of difficulty in the rail industry is the wave of bankruptcies that has engulfed a number of major carriers, beginning in the modern era with the New York, Ontario and Western in 1959. Later victims included the Penn Central, the Rock Island, and the Milwaukee Road, along with a number of smaller lines. Although bankruptcies are not new to the rail industry,[2] the bankruptcies of the modern era led to abandonments of service on a significant scale in many areas of the country.

Less dramatic but also important from the standpoint of service losses is the abandonment of routes by financially sound carriers. With the loosening of national regulation of the railroads, a number of carriers began to abandon lines that were no longer profitable. That trend was reinforced by mergers that became easier after deregulation. When formerly competing carriers merge, the new company may find that

123

some of its lines duplicate one another. Abandonment of those lines often follows.

The combined effects of bankruptcies and abandonments can be seen in the decline of the nation's rail mileage from 249,433 miles in 1929 to 184,500 miles in 1979, a decline of approximately 26 percent.[3] Many communities that formerly had rail service no longer do, and other areas previously served by two or more rail carriers are now served by one.

The current difficulties of the railroads have been attributed to a variety of causes. One widely cited factor is that the system was over-built, especially in the Northeast.[4] Most of the nation's system was constructed before the creation of an extensive highway system and the development of reliable air transportation. As the roads and airways grew in capacity, rail systems in some areas became unnecessarily large relative to the rail traffic that remained.

Another contributing element is exhaustion of natural resources along lines built to tap them and the closing of other businesses that generated traffic for the railroads.[5] If a line's chief customer is a textile firm that subsequently closes, the line may become superfluous. Once coal deposits are exhausted, a line built to haul coal will be in serious trouble. To the extent that current contractions in the rail system are due to these factors, the contractions are not causes for alarm but indications of normal economic adjustments.

A number of observers, however, contend that government policies have caused much of the "railroad problem." The difficulties of the railroads have been blamed on heavy government subsidies to competing transportation modes, including air and water transport and highway-based modes.[6] In a related vein, government regulations have sometimes required railroads to provide uneconomical services,[7] adding to their financial difficulties. According to this perspective, government action is essential for solving at least some of the railroads' problems.

Contractions in the nation's rail system are significant because of the importance of transportation for economic growth and development.[8] Recent research confirms the value of transportation investments as a means of stimulating economic growth.[9] While almost all products can be shipped by modes other than rail, railroads have cost advantages for a number of commodities,[10] and state and local officials fear that abandonments will choke off future economic development.[11]

In a broader perspective, continuing instability in the Middle East underscores the dangers of reliance on petroleum-intensive transportation modes such as trucks and airplanes. Less dramatically, dwindling U.S. and world oil supplies suggest a future need for transportation systems that can function with little or no petroleum. As experience in

Europe and Japan indicates, electrified rail systems can move large quantities of freight (and large numbers of people) without immense oil consumption.[12] If that is what the future holds, the transition will be far more traumatic if the current rail system is largely scrapped and then must be built again.

The States Respond

States facing a loss of rail freight service have a number of options to prevent the loss. An old approach dating back to the nineteenth century[13] is the subsidization of rail service to prevent abandonments, permit capital improvements, and prop up financially ailing carriers. Subsidies can take the form of outright grants or loans provided on generous terms.

A second approach, also very old, is the use of tax reductions to encourage preservation of rail service.[14] Since state and local taxes consume a fairly large share of net railway income,[15] tax reductions can be a significant form of aid.

A third and more drastic method for preserving rail service is direct state ownership of railroads. The publicly owned railroad can be government operated, leased to a private carrier, or simply preserved for future use if current traffic is limited but expected to grow in the future.[16] Preservation of a line without operating it, "rail banking," is an outgrowth of the fact that maintaining an existing line is normally much less expensive than permitting the line to be dismantled and then rebuilding it. Given the American preference for free-enterprise approaches, at least at a symbolic level, public ownership of railroads is likely to be seen as a last resort for preserving rail service.

Information on state programs to preserve rail freight service was gathered through a mail survey of state transportation officials. The survey was conducted during the spring and summer of 1983 and produced a response rate of 95.9 percent.[17] The high response rate can be attributed to the short questionnaire (one page); the inclusion of a stamped self-addressed return envelope; the use of three follow-ups, each with a copy of the questionnaire; and the interest of the respondents in the issue.[18]

The survey returns indicated substantial state activity in rail freight service preservation. Twenty-one states reported some type of rail preservation effort, with nine states adopting subsidies and eight states having tax relief programs. Seventeen reported public ownership of one or more railroads (some states have more than one program).[19] The analysis that follows will seek to explain adoption of public ownership (see Table 10.1).

TABLE 10.1. ■ States that own railroads

Connecticut	Oklahoma
Delaware	Pennsylvania
Maryland	South Dakota
Massachusetts	Tennessee
Michigan	Vermont
Mississippi	Washington[b]
New Hampshire	West Virginia
New Jersey[a]	Wisconsin
Ohio	

NOTE: As of summer 1983, Georgia and Rhode Island did not respond to the survey. Hawaii was not surveyed.

[a]Right of way for passenger service; negotiations for freight use in progress.

[b]Port authority.

Contrary to the common impression that goverment programs tend to be extraordinarily large and expensive, the publicly owned rail lines generally convey an image of thrift and economy.[20] Most are comparatively short; many are less than 30 miles. Shorter lines are less costly to maintain, other things being equal, and can therefore survive with few resources. There are some exceptions to the shortness tendency, such as the Vermont Railway, which has nearly 130 miles of track, but most of the state-owned lines conform to the pattern.[21]

Another sign of thrift and economy is the locomotive fleets, which are typically small and far from new. To take an extreme case, the Towanda-Monroeton Shippers Lifeline uses track owned by the Pennsylvania Department of Transportation. That railroad's only locomotive was built before World War II. The Ashtabula, Carson, and Jefferson Railroad, owned by Ohio, has a single locomotive nearly forty years old.[22]

Note too that public ownership does not necessarily bring public operation. A number of the publicly owned lines are operated by private firms. The use of a private operating company can help to restrain costs by introducing an element of competition; different firms may compete for the opportunity to operate a line.[23] In addition, if and when ownership of a publicly owned line is returned to private hands, a public operating agency would have to be dismantled, a traumatic process at best. Reliance on a private operator can help to reduce that trauma.

Influences on Decisions

One influence on state decisions regarding public ownership of railroads involves orientations toward the use of government power, as well as the broader political and administrative climate. Transportation decisions may be shaped by ideological forces, particularly those involving the proper role of government in resolving social problems and managing the economy.[24] Ideological liberalism, with its greater acceptance of governmental activism, should provide a more congenial environment for public ownership. Conservatives are likely to prefer letting market forces take their course, even if that results in the abandonment of service to some areas. Because preservation programs have not been a particularly salient issue for the general public, party ideologies may be particularly important in determining responses to proposals for public ownership.

Rail policies may also reflect the influence of administrative arrangements. Organizational structures shape the perspectives of decision makers, particularly administrators, who are naturally concerned with preserving the importance of their agencies. At the same time, organizational structures may enchance or diminish the access of groups to the decision-making process.[25] If a state lacks a department of transportation, its chief transportation agency is likely to be the highway department, an agency where transportation problems are likely to be viewed in terms of highways. In that case, individuals who are concerned with highway issues are likely to be welcome, but people concerned with other transportation needs may receive a less cordial reception. By contrast, a department of transportation, particularly one with jurisdiction over railroads, is likely to have a broader perspective on transportation issues and to be more receptive to people concerned with a loss of rail service. Both circumstances should provide an environment more supportive of rail preservation programs, including public ownership.

Another political influence on rail programs may be Conrail. Policy researchers have often found that state officials look to other governments for guidance in dealing with policy problems.[26] Borrowing existing programs helps to reduce the uncertainty associated with innovation and requires much less effort than inventing a new approach. The establishment of Conrail may have provided a cue to state officials regarding the need for rail preservation and a technique for achieving it. In addition, Conrail may have enhanced the political acceptability of state involvement by establishing a precedent for government intervention.

Although the example of Conrail is available to all state officials, the presence of Conrail in a state is likely to be especially significant for its officials. First, officials in such a state can point to Conrail as evidence of the need for and suitability of public ownership in their state. Second, since officials have many issues and problems clamoring for their attention, officials in states where Conrail operates are more likely to notice its existence and therefore the problem to which it was a response.

A different perspective on innovation holds that slack resources are the main cause of innovation. Public ownership of a rail line involves acquisition costs, which can be considerable, and operating costs. In addition, acquisition of one line may set a precedent that leads to acquisition of other lines, a process that brings further expenses. Officials in relatively poor states may fear the immediate costs of public ownership and the longer-term costs even more. Prosperity will make the costs of public ownership easier to bear and should therefore encourage adoption of public ownership.

The problem environment may also influence state decisions regarding public ownership. The problem environment has a number of potentially significant aspects, one of which is the geographical distribution of the population. A number of studies have found that states with high urbanization and population density spend relatively less on highways than sparsely populated states.[27] A dispersed population requires more roads and enormous amounts of money and effort to meet the needs of road and highway transportation. As a result, little money or effort is likely to remain for other transportation programs. In this view, states acting to support rail service are likely to be relatively metropolitan and densely populated.

Population distributions may also influence rail policies by virtue of the economies of rail transportation. Many analysts believe the railroads have relatively high fixed costs.[28] Rail transportation will therefore be more economical with high traffic volume, a situation most likely to occur with concentrated populations. Where the population is relatively dispersed, traffic is also likely to be dispersed, making rail transportation relatively inefficient. If officials try to allocate resources in the most productive ways, densely populated states should display greater acitivity in rail preservation.

The relative prominence of businesses that are particularly dependent on rail transportation is another important aspect of the problem environment. The transportation literature indicates that the bulk of rail freight traffic consists of minerals, farm products, food, chemicals, metal products, and manufactured goods.[29] Where these economic sectors provide a larger share of state income, state officials may have more concern for rail preservation and therefore be more likely to adopt preservation programs, including public ownership. States where few firms are likely to ship by rail have less to lose from the abandonment of rail lines, at least in the short run, and may be less receptive to preservation programs.

An alternative theory holds that where a state's economy is heavily reliant on products normally shipped by rail, the railroads will be better able to maintain profitable operation. In that event, government assistance will be less necessary and may therefore be less common, assuming that assistance programs are a response to needs rather than exertion of railroad influence. According to this perspective, states where relatively few firms rely on rail transportation are likely to have more lines threatened with abandonment and consequently face more pressure to adopt preservation programs.

The nature of the state's rail system is yet another important facet of the problem environment. In states with very extensive rail systems, officials may feel that their rail service is sufficient to make preservation unnecessary. Where rail systems are small, particularly relative to land area, officials may feel a greater need for preservation programs to maintain a scarce resource. In a related fashion, states experiencing major contractions in their rail systems may be stimulated to enact public ownership programs, regardless of the absolute size of the system. In this view, public ownership is a reaction to abandonments, a form of crisis innovation. Communities anticipating service losses, businesses fearing the loss of rail access, and state officials concerned for the state economy are likely to see abandonments as a serious threat demanding action.

An alternative possibility is that preservation programs are simply a function of railroads as an interest group seeking benefits from government. Public ownership helps to preserve railroading jobs, provides connecting traffic for other railroads, and may help rail lines shed unprofitable routes with less opposition. In this view, where railroads are politically powerful, they are likely to press for public ownership to ensure that they continue to produce benefits, but at the taxpayers' expense. Two plausible indicators of railroad influence are railroad employment (because of the value of numbers as an interest-group resource) and railroad payrolls (because of the value of economic resources in exerting influence).[30] In this view, public ownership does not reflect railroad problems but railroad infuence.

Analysis

Preliminary analysis supports some of the initial hypotheses. Public ownership is concentrated in states with relatively liberal political parties, but the existence and scope of a department of transportation is essentially unrelated to publicly owned railroads.

States where Conrail operates are more likely to have public ownership, as expected. A note of caution is in order, however: Conrail's creation was a response to abandonments. Its apparent influence may reflect the nature of the problem environment, at least to some degree, rather than emulation (see Table 10.2).

TABLE 10.2. ■ State characteristics and public ownership of freight railroads

	Public ownership[a]
Republican party ideology[b]	.27[g]
Democratic party ideology[c]	−.27[g]
DOT score[d]	.13
Conrail[e]	.49[h]
Median income	−.09
Percent metropolitan	.09
Population density	.45[h]
Rail commodities[f]	−.17
Rail mileage, 1978	−.28[g]
Track mileage per 1,000 sq. miles	.28[g]
1978 mileage/1963 mileage	−.59[h]
Railroad employment	−.08
Railroad payroll	−.08

[a]Coefficients are Pearson's r's.

[b]McGregor, 1978: 1020–1021; high scores denote liberalism.

[c]McGregor, 1978: 1022–1023; low scores denote liberalism.

[d]0 = no department of transportation; 1 = DOT excludes railroads; 2 = DOT includes railroads.

[e]Conrail operates in state.

[f]Value of mineral production, crops, livestock, food, chemicals, metal products, machinery, electrical equipment, transportation machinery, groceries, and motor vehicles as a percentage of total state income, 1977.

[g]Significant at the .05 level.

[h]Significant at the .01 level.

The evidence at the zero-order level does not support the slack-resources model. Median income is of no value in explaining adoption of public ownership. The small size and modest facilities of many state-owned lines may put them in the price range of poorer as well as wealthier states.

The problem environment fares somewhat unevenly in accounting for patterns of state ownership. Metropolitanization and the value of commodities likely to be shipped by rail are essentially unrelated to decisions regarding public ownership. However, public ownership is concentrated in more densely populated states, as expected. States with smaller rail systems are more likely to adopt public ownership, as expected, but the opposite tendency results when the size of the rail system is adjusted for land area. Public ownership is strongly concentrated in states whose rail systems have shrunk in recent years, as suggested by the crisis innovation model. However, public ownership is unrelated to railroad employment and payrolls.

Discriminant analysis of public ownership produces findings consistent with the crisis innovation model and suggests policy-making that reacts to a problem rather than acting from internal direction. States adopting public ownership have experienced proportionally large declines in their rail systems from 1963 to 1978. That single variable correctly predicts the decisions of 85 percent of the states. No other state characteristic examined in this analysis could significantly improve the fit of the model (see Table 10.3).

TABLE 10.3. ■ Discriminant analysis of state ownership of railroads

Standardized canonical discriminant function coefficient: 1978 rail mileage divided by 1963 mileage $= 1.00$	Canonical correlation $= .58$ Wilks's lambda $= .66$ % correctly classified $= 85.1$ Chi$^2 = 17.8$[a]
Group centroids[b]: Group 0 $= .533$; Group 1 $= -.909$	

[a]Significant at the .0001 level with d.f.
[b]Group 0 = state lacks program; group 1 = state has program.

The results of the discriminant analysis are consistent with other evidence on publicly owned railroads. A number of the lines owned by state (and local) governments were originally owned by private railroads that became unwilling or financially unable to continue service. The threatened loss of service and the lack of a private-sector alternative led to public ownership to ensure continued service.[31] Not all of the publicly owned lines fit that pattern but many do.

Public ownership is not the only option available to state policymakers who face the loss of rail service. Subsidies and tax relief programs have also been adopted in some states. Although the evidence is not completely clear, adoption of those comparatively modest preservation programs appears to reflect the same influences as many other routine state decisions: Subsidies and tax relief programs tend to be found in states with comparatively liberal Republican parties and either high population density or high metropolitanization.[32] Public ownership appears to be more closely linked to the problem environment, as indicated by contractions in the state railroad system.

Conclusion

The states have often been criticized for failing to deal with a wide variety of problems facing American society. In a similar (and related) fashion, critics charge that incrementalism isolates decision makers from environmental changes and problems.[33] The results of this analysis indicate that policymakers are able to move beyond the restraints of incremental routines and respond to environmental changes, at least occasionally.

Under crisis conditions, the estimated costs of failing to deal with the situation quickly are high. Policymakers are therefore likely to think that higher decision costs are worth paying, at least compared to routine decisions. More policy options can be considered. At the same time, because the crisis is perceived to entail great costs if it is not resolved, policymakers are more willing to bear the uncertainty that major policy shifts bring.

Because crises generate demands for action, the fear that major policy changes will create political antagonisms is offset by the fear that failing to act will create political antagonisms. In short, the crisis environment breaks down the forces that support incremental decision making.

State willingness to take the bold step of public ownership may reflect in part the potential economic benefits of rail preservation. A loss of service may reduce future economic growth, a prospect that many officials find disturbing. Whether other policy problems that do not threaten economic loss, not to mention inconvenience to the business community, would provoke equally bold responses is far from clear.

Adoption of rail preservation programs has undoubtedly been facilitated by the states' traditionally large role in transportation policy generally. In addition, rail programs dating back to the nineteenth century provide ample historical precedent for action. Without these conditional factors, not to mention the national government's creation of Conrail and Amtrak, the states might very well have proceeded more cautiously.

Of course, a crisis must be perceived in order to stimulate major policy changes. The bankruptcy of a major railroad or the abandonment of a rail line is a visible, sometimes dramatic event. Faced with the visible threatened loss of service, state officials have responded with the crisis innovation of public ownership.

NOTES

See Bibliography for full reference.

1. Hollingsworth and Whitehouse (1977: 28–37).
2. Drury (1985: 11).
3. *Yearbook* (1981: 46).
4. Bowersox, Calabro, and Wagenheim (1981: 77); Conant (1964: 116); Keeler (1983: 123–124).
5. Conant (1964: 115–116).
6. Hollingsworth and Whitehouse (1977: 33–34); Pegrum (1973: 69).
7. Hollingsworth and Whitehouse (1977: 33–34); Coyle, Bardi, and Cavinato (1982: 308).
8. Locklin (1972: 16); Sampson and Farris (1979: 5).
9. Dye (1980).
10. Keeler (1983: 76).
11. Black and Runke (1975: 20, 46).
12. See Alston (1984); Creger and Combs (1981).
13. Grant and Nixon (1975: 495); Stover (1961: 89); Black and Runke (1975: 54).
14. Black and Runke (1975: 5, 55, 91).
15. Black and Runke (1975: 86); Thompson (1981).
16. Black and Runke (1975: 5, 61–62).
17. Hawaii was not included in the survey because it lacks public rail service.
18. See Bailey (1982: 164–177); Backstrom and Hursh-Cesar (1981: 118).
19. See Nice (1987b).
20. Lewis (1986); Nice (1987a).
21. Lewis (1986: 217).
22. Lewis (1986: 24, 209).
23. Lewis (1986); Nice (1987a).
24. See Colcord (1979: 3, 14).
25. Edwards and Sharkansky (1978: 121); Seidman (1975: 14–15).
26. Sharkansky (1970: chapter 6); Walker (1969).
27. Dye (1966: 157–161); Dye (1981: 431); Friedman (1971: 518); Sharkansky and Hofferbert (1971: 339).
28. Pegrum (1973: 168–169); Sampson and Farris (1979: 59).
29. Bowersox, Calabro, and Wagenheim (1981: 69); *Economic ABZs* (1980: table IV-10); Pegrum (1973: 28).
30. Greenwald (1977: 330–331); Ornstein and Elder (1978: 71–74).
31. See Lewis (1986); Nice (1987a).
32. Nice (1987b).
33. Sharkansky (1970: 51, 65–68).

11

Conclusions

Introduction

The preceding chapters have examined patterns of adopting a variety of policy innovations. Drawing on insights from the innovation literature and the literature on policy-making generally, the analyses explored the roles of the problem environment, resource availability, and orientations toward governmental power and change in shaping innovation decisions. This chapter will explore the findings across the various innovations.

The innovations examined here do not constitute a representative sample of policy innovations. The patterns of findings that emerge should be regarded as only suggestive. An overview of the possible eccentricities of the innovations analyzed will help place the results in a broader perspective.

The Problem Environment

Perhaps the most striking pattern to emerge from the preceding chapters is the prominence of the problem environment in explaining innovation decisions. Teacher competency testing is concentrated in states with a history of relatively low education performance, a circumstance likely to produce demands for improvements. Sunset legislation is generally found in states with comparatively weak governmental institutions; incentives to improve institutional capacity are likely to be stronger in those states. Contrary to expectations, however, divided partisan control, which might spur legislative efforts to control the executive branch, was negatively related to adoption of sunset laws.

The two transportation innovations, ownership of freight railroads and subsidies of Amtrak service, both reflect the influence of the problem environment, although in different ways. State-owned freight lines are largely a function of contractions in rail systems. Communities and businesses threatened with loss of rail service due to abandonments or bankruptcies have pressed for public intervention, and a number of states have responded. Subsidies of Amtrak service can be explained with considerable accuracy by two of the most fundamental characteristics of the transportation task environment. Subsidizing states tend to have large populations, which are needed to generate substantial traffic volume, and large land areas, which may enhance the salience of transportation programs in view of the greater distances to be overcome.

The problem environment facing elected officials emerges as one force shaping decisions regarding public finance of election campaigns. Greater Republican party dominance in state politics tends to blunt the impact of Republican liberalism on enactment of public finance programs. Greater Republican dominance is likely to make Republican fund-raising easier, and a number of studies indicate that Republican candidates are particularly helped by campaign spending. If Republicans are reluctant to enact a public finance system where they are electorally dominant, an action that would reduce a significant advantage for Republican candidates, they are displaying the same desire for self-preservation that other officials often display.

The role of the problem environment in shaping the other innovations is less clear. State calls for a national balanced budget amendment have undoubtedly grown from the persistent national budget deficits; in that respect, the calls are a response to a problem. However, the distribution of state responses displays no visible relationship to various state aspects of the problem context. Whether states labor under similar requirements or are relatively successful or unsuccessful in obtaining federal aid tells us little about how these states are likely to react to national budget issues.

At the zero-order level, state-financed property tax programs emphasizing need are concentrated in states with high tax effort, but the relationship reverses in the multivariate analysis. On balance, the evidence does not provide clear support for the view that higher property taxes lead to adoption of more general state-financed relief. Similarly, ambiguous findings result from analysis of deregulation of sodomy. The concept of the problem environment is particularly hazy in this instance; whether sodomy is a problem is a matter of considerable controversy.

Overall, the analyses produce clear evidence of the influence of the problem environment on five of the eight innovations included in this study. In several cases the nature of the problems may help to account for their impact. Educational performance can be measured by a variety of standardized instruments that give at least a broad indication of how well states are doing.[1] A poorly performing educational system is likely to produce large numbers of irate parents, some likely to communicate that displeasure to public officials. A poorly educated labor force may also hamper state efforts to attract new businesses and industries. In short, the consequences of a poor performance are likely to be felt by some sensitive nerves, and performance can be documented with a fair degree of accuracy.

In a similar manner, contractions in a state's railroad system are relatively visible and easy to verify. Major abandonments and bankruptcies often attract considerable publicity, and even small contractions attract the attention of the communities affected. The loss of rail service often creates fears of low future economic growth.[2] Once again, a problem that can be readily measured and carries painful consequences spurs innovation.

The other transportation innovation examined in this study, subsidies of Amtrak service, also reflects the problem environment. The transportation field includes a large number of concrete indicators of need and performance: passenger volume, traffic fatalities, fuel consumption, labor costs, and so forth. Although Amtrak has been embroiled in controversy for much of its existence, the basic criteria for determining the appropriateness of passenger rail service are fairly well established. The states have a long history of involvement in transportation policy-making, and the combination of a recognized responsibility, clear measures of need and performance, and established criteria regarding suitability of service help to link the problem environment and innovation decisions.

Sunset legislation presents a somewhat more ambiguous case. Legislative oversight of the bureaucracy is a broadly recognized responsibility, although controversies regarding specific legislative efforts in that regard abound. Measuring the extent of legislative control over the bureaucracy, however, is a difficult task. Legislators may feel that they are influential when agencies are actually quite autonomous or may feel frustration when agencies actually comply with legislative directives to a considerable degree. Moreover, although legislative control of the bureaucracy is broadly recognized as legitimate, at least in general, sunset laws mingle that responsibility with the possible termination of many programs. Not surprisingly, the results of the analysis are less than fully clear; indicators of the problem environment are related to sunset provisions, but those indicators may be capturing orientations toward governmental power as well.

The state role in conducting elections is firmly established, and one facet of that role is the regulation of campaign finance. For many years, the problem environment posed major measurement problems. Campaign finance records for most of our history were incomplete at best and in some cases misleading. Recent reforms have produced more accurate records as well as an outpouring of research on campaign finance and the effects of campaign spending. Policymakers have gained a much clearer image of the problem environment and its implications for their careers. Not surprisingly, career concerns are reflected in decisions regarding public finance.

The other three innovations examined in this study do not produce clear evidence of the influence of the problem enviroment, and all three share a common feature: The nature and even the existence of a problem is very much a matter of controversy. National budget deficits have been widely condemned in recent years, particularly by the officials who prepare and enact the budgets. Whether the national government should have the option of running a deficit to stimulate the economy is highly controversial. In addition, if the deficits helped spur the economic recovery from the 1982 recession, even they may not deserve complete condemnation. In that context, the problem environment may not help to explain state responses to the issue.

The property tax has been similarly controversial. Economists have reached varying conclusions regarding the incidence of the property tax; the need for relief is therefore uncertain. The unpopularity of the property tax has been amply documented, but demands on state and local treasuries are high, and broad-ranging relief can be very costly. In that context, the problem environment does not provide clear guidance to policymakers.

The problem environment is even more amorphous in the case of sodomy laws, which in most cases cover the conduct of married couples. Whether and when that behavior constitutes a problem is highly controversial, as is the issue of whether it is a governmental responsibility. The evidence suggests that perceptions of the problem environment play a role in shaping responses. Reliable indicators of the problem environment itself are lacking in this case, however.

Overall, the innovations examined here involved areas generally recognized as public responsibilities in the past; none of the innovations constituted an entry into a previously nongovernmental domain, although some did represent novel extensions of an established responsibility, as in public finance of campaigns. The element that seems to distinguish the innovations with the clearest evidence of responding to the problem environment from the other innovations is goal agreement. Improved educational performance, mobility for freight and passengers, bureaucratic accountability to elected officials, and fair elections are goals with fairly broad support. People may disagree over precise specifications of the goals and how to achieve them, but the general goals have fairly broad appeal. In that context, the basis for a response to the problem environment is established, although not necessarily with ease.

The other innovations present a rather different picture. The ideal or fair distribution of the tax burden is a matter of considerable disagreement, with the possible exception of the desire to have one's own tax bill lowered. Whether a particular distribution or level is a problem is consequently difficult to establish. Conceptions of ideal or normal sexual behavior are similarly diverse. Is homosexuality a mental illness, a sin, or a legitimate lifestyle? Is sex to be used for procreation, expression of love, or simple sensory gratification? Faced with a variety of different answers, officials may have a difficult time deciding whether a problem exists, much less grasping its precise nature.

The national budget deficit does not seem to fit the above pattern, at least at first glance. Certainly something that has been so widely condemned seems to imply a clear goal, but appearances may be misleading. In the absence of a clear prospect that economic growth will eliminate the deficit, two painful options remain: raising additional revenue and cutting spending.[3] The apparently clear goal of reducing the deficit grows hazy when linked to the goals of avoiding tax increases and maintaining benefits. Moreover, the consequences of a national balanced budget amendment for individual states are far from clear. A state's officials might feel that their congressional delegation could shield their state from budget cuts and shift new revenue burdens elsewhere. Indeed, state officials might enact a resolution calling for a balanced budget amendment while believing that the amendment would never pass. The enactment could be largely for symbolic or public relations purposes, a phenomenon that has been observed in a variety of settings.[4] The clear, broadly shared goal appears on closer inspection to dissolve. The problem environment consequently has little explanatory power.

Problems that are linked to broadly shared goals, then, are likely to stimulate policy innovations. In policy areas where goals are in conflict with one another or are the subject of considerable disagreement, problems may be less likely to foster innovation. In the latter context, the existence of a problem is likely to be a matter of uncertainty or dispute.

Advocates of the competing goals may produce conflicting recommendations for an appropriate response, and the many veto points of the policy-making process will take a heavy toll on significant changes if they have no other bases for support. Innovations that do emerge from that context may well be due to forces other than the problem environment.

The prominence of problems in accounting for several innovations examined here stands in marked contrast to the view that public policies are simply an outgrowth of the internal machinations of government and lack any discernible connection to real-world conditions. As noted in Chapter 2, there are many ways in which problems may go undetected or be misunderstood, and governmental officials and institutions are not neutral instruments for registering or responding to problems. Nevertheless, public policies do bear the imprint of the problem environment, at least occasionally.

Resources

Although the innovation literature places considerable emphasis on resources as a major influence on innovation,[5] the innovations examined here do not generally support the slack-resources hypothesis. At the zero-order level, wealthier states are more likely to subsidize Amtrak service, a policy that entails direct costs, and to deregulate sodomy, a policy that does not. Neither relationship survives controls for other variables, however.

Affluence is of no value in accounting for state ownership of freight railroads, in spite of the costs of ownership. As noted earlier, though, most of the publicly owned lines are quite modest operations and do not generate great costs.

Wealth is similarly unsuccessful in explaining decisions regarding property tax relief, a program with significant potential costs. That somewhat surprising result may be a function of two factors. First, while poorer states may have more people in need of tax relief (depending on the true distribution of the property tax burden), the ease of financing relief is greater in wealthier states. The inverse relationship between needs and ability to finance may mean that the two forces offset one another, yielding little overall relationship between wealth and tax relief. Second, to the degree that relief programs reduce taxpayer unrest, the programs may be approximately self-financing in a political sense. That is, the adoption of a relief program may reduce taxpayer resistance to taxes in general and make raising revenues through other mechanisms easier. A state would not need to be wealthy to take advantage of that phenomenon.

Wealth is also unrelated to adoption of public finance of campaigns. As with publicly owned railroads, however, the state campaign finance systems are typically modest operations. They generally cover only a few offices and rarely pay more than a small fraction of campaign costs. A limited system is probably within the means of any state if the inclination is present.

The most striking findings for the slack-resources pespective are the negative relationships between wealth, on one hand, and adoptions of competency testing, sunset laws, and resolutions for a national budget amendment. At the zero-order level, the innovative states in these three areas tend to be poorer than other states, although none of those relationships survives controls for other variables. All three innovations can be adopted at a modest cost. In the immediate sense, calling for a national budget amendment entails no costs, although its impact on national grants to states and localities could be painful. Sunset laws can be implemented at negligible cost if reviews are conducted at a very basic level and bring hopes of long-run cost savings (that may or may not materialize).

Teacher competency testing entails higher potential costs, but their claims on the state treasury can be minimized by using off-the-shelf tests and charging a testing fee. Testing emerges as a comparatively inexpensive educational reform when contrasted with higher teacher salaries, smaller classes, specialized personnel for students with learning problems or exceptional capabilities, additional equipment, and so forth. A program that entails some expenses may still appear to be a money saver if the likely alternatives are even more expensive.

The limited impact of the resource environment overall may be a reflection of several factors. First, as noted above, the innovations analyzed here do not in general involve large direct costs. The creation of a university system or an extensive freeway system, either of which would involve enormous start-up costs and a large, continuing financial commitment, might be much more affected by resource availability than the innovations studies here. Second, the growth of associations of state and local officials, both nationwide (now roughly one hundred associations)[6] and regional, as well as think tanks, interest groups, and the media have significantly reduced the costs of searching for potential innovations and analyzing them. Conferences, journals, newsletters, and policy entrepreneurs spread information about proposals to states poor in resources as well as the richer. Third, a number of the innovations examined here carry the promise of future economic benefits or cost savings. A better-educated labor force may help a state attract new businesses and industries. Transportation maintenance and improvements may have a similar effect. Sunset laws may help to control the costs of government. Whether any of these benefits will actually result is, of course, problematic, but the promise of future economic gains or cost savings may help to sever the link between resources and innovations. Certainly the claim that a program will pay for itself is a firmly established political tactic.[7]

Orientations toward Governmental Change

The expectation that ideological liberalism, with its confidence in progress, belief in analysis, and acceptance of a broader public role, should be a consistent force for policy innovation, while conservatism should consistently discourage innovation in light of conservatives' suspicion of governmental activism and preference for traditional ways, is not consistently supported by the evidence. At the zero-order level, five innovations are particularly common in states with comparatively liberal political parties, liberal electorates, or a history of innovativeness. Only three innovations are concentrated in states characterized by conservatism, traditionalism, or a history of being slow to adopt innovations.

Publicly owned freight railroads are concentrated in states with relatively liberal political parties, as are tax relief programs emphasizing need, publicly fiananced campaigns, Amtrak subsidies, and laws permitting sodomy. More liberal electorates and a history of innovativeness seem to provide a congenial environment for tax relief, subsidies of Amtrak, and deregulation of sodomy. The moralistic culture, with its broad view of public responsibilities and emphasis on honest government, tends to foster adoption of publicly financed campaigns.

Some of the zero-order relationships present a very different pattern, however. Teacher testing, sunset laws, and calls for a national budget amendment are generally found in states with conservative parties. States with competency testing have generally been slow to adopt innovations, as have states adopting sunset laws. Competency-testing states tend to have traditional cultures, and states calling for a budget amendment generally have conservative electorates. The drift of the zero-order relationships, then, is mixed but shows more innovations conforming to the liberalism-innovativeness perspective than not.

The multivariate findings, however, show a more even balance across the ideological spectrum. Three innovations (state-financed tax relief, public finance of campaigns, and deregulation of sodomy) are associated with ideologically liberal political parties. Public finance of campaigns also tends to be found in states with moralistic cultures, which emphasize honest politics. By contrast, traditionalistic states, with their emphasis on hierarchical control, tend to have teacher testing, and calls for a national amendment come disproportionately from states with conservative electorates. Although the findings regarding sunset laws are not clear-cut, the relationships are consistent with the view that sunset legislation reflects an underlying opposition to activist government.

While the multivariate findings are only suggestive, they indicate that the compatibility of a specific innovation with prevailing ideological or cultural orientations is likely to be important in shaping that innovation's prospects for adoption. Generalized liberalism, by contrast, does not appear to be a dependable source of subsequent innovations in general, although liberalism is associated with adoption of innovations consistent with liberal ideology.

Specifically, state-financed tax relief, with its targeting of aid to poorer individuals, de facto targeting of funds to poorer higher-tax-rate localities, and ability to reduce resistance to local revenue raising pursues three goals consistent with liberal ideologies. Conservatives, reluctant to redistribute incomes and skeptical of government activism, are likely to be less enthusiastic about state-financed relief. An innovation consistent with liberal goals finds a warmer response in more liberal states.

In a similar vein, public finance of campaigns can help to equalize the resources available to candidates and reduce the inequality of influence produced by private finance. Liberalism, with its emphasis on equality, provides a more receptive environment for an innovation of that type.

Finally, liberalism's greater acceptance of alternative lifestyles provides a more favorable climate for deregulation of sodomy. Conservatism, with its greater willingness to preserve traditional values and practices, even if that preservation requires govermental support, is less compatible with the innovation of legalized sodomy.

The innovations associated with various aspects of conservatism or traditionalism at the multivariate level display compatibility with the values embedded in those belief systems. Conservatives generally regard a balanced budget as essential in achieving fiscal prudence. If officials can spend money without raising revenues, conservatives believe, expenditures are unlikely to receive the scrutiny they deserve. Not surprisingly, ideologically conservative states are more likely to have passed resolutions calling for a national budget amendment.

Cultural traditionalism is likely to foster adoption of teacher testing in at least two ways. First, traditionalism emphasizes hierarchical control. Competency testing has generally been imposed on educators over their strong objections; a culture that tolerates or encourages hierarchical control rather than decision making based on consultation or bargaining facilitates adoption of innovations imposed on subordinates. Second, traditionalism, with its emphasis on preserving the past and preference for a relatively limited government role, is likely to incline decision makers toward educational reforms that make few demands on the public or the public treasury, reforms like competency testing, rather than reforms that could be more expensive or require broader social changes.

The somewhat ambiguous findings regarding sunset laws are consistent with the view that they spring from a generally antigovernment orientation. Conservative Democratic parties, a history of being slow to adopt new programs, low spending levels, and weak governmental institutions, are hardly consistent with a commitment to activist government. Sunset laws, with their accompanying prospect of program terminations, are broadly compatible with an antigovernment orientation.

Reflections on the Study of Innovations

The preceding analysis suggests that much can be gained from studying a variety of innovations within a broadly comparable analytical framework. Although general inclinations regarding innovativeness, averaged across a number of innovations, have considerable analytical value, exploration of the forces surrounding individual innovations can greatly enrich our understanding of the policy-making process. Analyzing individual innovations is particularly critical for understanding the roles of the problem environment and ideological-cultural forces in shaping innovations. A transportation problem may influence adoption of transportation innovations but is unlikely to help account for innovations in welfare, education, or public personnel administration. Conservative ideologies may encourage enactment of innovations that pursue conservative goals, discourage enactment of liberal proposals, and make no difference regarding nonideological innovations. Those effects are likely to be lost if all types of innovations are combined into a composite innovation score.

The unexpectedly limited role of the resource environment in accounting for innovation decisions is, on reflection, not too surprising. First, as noted earlier, none of these innovations is particularly costly, at least when compared to the overall size of the typical state budget. Innovations with greater start-up and continuation costs would probably be more affected by resource availability. Second, the variation among the states in resource availability has declined over the years,[8] with the result that the resource advantages of the wealthier states are smaller now than in the past. Not surprisingly, then, the explanatory powers of resources and socioeconomic factors in state policy-making have declined.[9] A more varied resource environment, such as that at the local level, could lead to a stronger relationship between resources and policy decisions.[10]

The limited impact of resources in accounting for the innovations examined here may also reflect the decision context surrounding individual innovations. For all practical purposes, all of the states have sufficient resources to support modestly priced policy innovations, although not necessarily with equal ease. In that context, the process of selecting innovations is unlikely to be random. Potential innovations feasible from a resource standpoint but have nothing else to recommend them are likely to be pushed aside by proposals that combine affordability with the promise of solving a pressing problem or pursuit of a broadly shared goal. Public officials, who are keenly aware of the need for plausible explanations of their actions,[11] are unlikely to regard "We can afford it" as a sufficient explanation. Unless a new initiative can be presented as solving a problem or pursuing a valued goal, officials may be reluctant to bear the costs and risks associated with innovation.[12]

The Comfort and the Discomfort of the Familiar

As noted in Chapter 1, there are typically many advantages on the side of current programs and practices. If officials are satisfied with current performance levels, they may have little inclination to search for alternative approaches. The costs of developing, evaluating, and enacting major policy changes, as well as investments in current systems, further discourage innovations. Major changes may provoke conflicts among officials or with administrative agencies or clientele. Dramatically different approaches may produce unanticipated results; maintaining the status quo generally involves much less uncertainty.

Current policies gain further strength when their deficiencies are not detected or are imperfectly understood. The obstacle course that new policies must run to reach enactment further reduces the prospects for innovation.[13] The promotion of innovation is likely to be an uphill struggle.

The numerous barriers facing the adoption of new approaches seem to suggest that nothing will ever change or that at most, changes will be modest and rare. From a broad perspective, however, changes in public policies and procedures have been widespread and in some cases dramatic.

The states have played a major role in the development of a system of higher education that includes some of the world's leading universities. The states have helped bring about sweeping changes in the nation's transportation system — changes that have made the automobile's dominance possible. State tax systems have shifted from heavy reliance on property taxation at the turn of the century to predominant reliance on consumption and income taxes, with state property taxes being virtually abandoned in most states.[14] State personnel systems have placed increased emphasis on expertise and ability and decreased emphasis on political affiliations in hiring, promoting, and firing employees. The states are active participants in a host of programs designed to fight poverty and illness; the changes in those programs since the 1920s have been immense by most standards. Racial minorities and women are treated far differently by many states than only a few decades ago.

These and many other changes have sometimes been bitterly resisted and have often occurred with a slowness that is extremely frustrating to advocates of change. Some changes have been adopted grudgingly, perhaps after goading by the national government or in response to financial inducements. A proposal may languish for years before the right combination of conditions makes its adoption possible.[15]

The breadth and extent of the changes indicate that although inertia is a powerful force in government, forces for change are sometimes stronger. While some people find stability and continuity sources of comfort and security, others grow bored with doing the same things and begin to think of new goals, strategies, and tactics. Curiosity and restlessness can be powerful antidotes to the status quo.

Even if current approaches are regarded as adequate in some overall sense, individuals with higher aspiration levels may still search for possible improvements. Their agitation for change is not necessarily welcome; they may even be regarded as troublemakers.[16] Their proposals are likely to encounter defeat, a result that will reinforce beliefs in the power of inertia.

The multiplicity of decision centers in the American political system, however, gives advocates of change many opportunities to gain a foothold. They can go from one decision-making arena to another until they find a sympathetic ear.[17] That search may include trying to find areas where the proposal is consistent with prevailing values and beliefs or areas with a serious problem that the proposal may help to resolve. Some may encounter a problem and then look for a solution; others develop a proposal first and then seek a problem in need of a solution.[18]

The large number of decision centers, coupled with the diversity of those centers, means that even though the odds that a single state will adopt a given innovation at a given time may be poor, the odds that some state may adopt it may be much greater. Nor are the advocates of a proposal limited to pressing their case at the state level. They may contact national and local officials in hopes of gaining a positive response.[19]

Once an innovation is adopted and put into practice, a number of factors may contribute to its diffusion to other jurisdictions. First, the uncertainty associated with a proposal declines as it accumulates a record in the field. A proposal may sound appealing in the abstract, but actual use may reveal unanticipated consequences. A program that has been tried and proved adequate is less risky than an untested proposal.

The uncertainty never disappears entirely. A program that is successful in one environment may fail in another. Differences in political climates, economic resources, and problem contexts may cause a program's performance to vary considerably. Moreover, the adoption and survival of a program in several states does not necessarily mean that it is successful. A program may have a variety of weaknesses that an inadequate evaluation might miss.

Note too that experience with a new program may eliminate uncertainty regarding that program with unflattering results. The program may prove to be ineffective, or it may arouse a storm of political controversy. Its costs may exceed initial estimates, and adverse side effects may develop. Looking before you leap sometimes leads to the decision not to leap.

If a new program seems to be successful in its early applications, other forces for diffusion may be set in motion. The associations of state and local officials distribute information on new approaches through conferences, newsletters, and other channels.[20] Personal contacts, interest groups, and news media also spread the word. The costs associated with discovering that new approach gradually decline for other states.

As word of a new approach spreads, people in other states may begin to press for its adoption. An education reform that promises improved educational opportunities; a tax reform that may produce a fairer distribution of the tax burden, at least in the eyes of some observers; or a transportation program that may bolster a sagging economy gradually becomes known. People who might benefit from those programs begin to ask their officials why they do not enjoy the benefits available in other states.

As experience with an innovation accumulates in some states, previously unsuccessful advocates of that innovation in other states may be encouraged to redouble their efforts. Advocates in states that are economically and politically similar to the adopters can point to their experience as evidence of the proposal's feasibility. As an innovation spreads, more and more states are likely to have role models that have adopted the program.

The growing awareness of the availability of a solution to a policy problem may also encourage officials to give the problem serious attention. Public officials are usually reluctant to raise an issue unless a solution is available.[21] The knowledge that officials in other states have experience with the program and can be contacted for guidance regarding implementation problems or adaptations to varying conditions may further allay fears of raising the issue.[22]

Resistance to change, then, can be overcome. Short-term organizational inertia does not necessarily mean long-term fossilization. State officials may quickly form beaten tracks to established programs and practices, but a fair number of those officials eventually explore other paths.

NOTES

See Bibliography for full reference.

1. The two measures that receive the greatest publicity, the SAT and the ACT, are not dependable indicators of system performance. They are taken by self-selected students, and a state's average score is heavily affected by the proportion of students taking the test and the composition of the test-taking group.

2. Black and Runke (1975: 20, 46).

3. Cutting spending is not always painful. Improved efficiency can cut costs with little or no pain to program beneficiaries. However, deficits of the magnitude reached during the early and mid-1980s could not in all likelihood be eliminated purely by efficiency improvements that do not affect program benefits.

4. Edelman (1964); Mayhew (1974).

5. Rogers (1983: 248–252); Sharkansky (1970: 182–183).

6. See Penne and Verduin (1986).

7. See Wildavsky (1974: 117–118).

8. Break (1980: 26–27).

9. Dye (1987: 308); Wright, Erikson, and McIver (1987).

10. See, for example, Worden and Worden (1986).

11. Kingdon (1981: 47–54).

12. Of course, the public explanation for a decision may bear little or no resemblance to the actual reasons for the decision. However, proposals that can readily be attached to a recognized problem or goal will be easier to explain than proposals requiring elaborate and convoluted rationales. To the degree that decision makers seek to limit the intellectual burdens of policy-making, proposals with relatively available, straightforward justifications will have a significant advantage over proposals that lack convenient, comprehensible justifications.

13. The decision-making processes of some private organizations are at least as com-

plex and filled with veto points as the legislative process in the typical state. The effect of discouraging innovations in those organizations is likely to resemble the public-sector tendency.

14. Maxwell and Aronson (1977: 17).

15. On the concept of policy windows, that combination of conditions that makes adoption possible, see Kingdon (1984: chapter 8).

16. Downs (1967: 275).

17. For a classic discussion of that phenonmenon, see Grodzins (1984: 274–276).

18. See Cohen, March, and Olsen (1972).

19. Nice (1987c: 22–24, 216).

20. Walker (1971: 894–895).

21. Peters (1986: 50).

22. Of course, officials are not completely free to ignore problems, but they do have some discretion in selecting agenda items.

BIBLIOGRAPHY

Aaron, Henry. 1975. *Who Pays the Property Tax?* Washington, D.C.: Brookings.

Aberbach, Joel. 1979. "Changes in Congressional Oversight." *American Behavioral Scientist* 22: 493–516.

Abraham, Henry. 1975. *The Judicial Process,* 3rd ed. New York: Oxford.

Adamany, David. 1972. *Campaign Finance in America.* North Scituate, Mass.: Duxbury.

Adamany, David, and George Agree. 1975. *Political Money.* Baltimore: Johns Hopkins.

Adrian, Charles. 1976. *State and Local Governments,* 4th ed. New York: McGraw-Hill.

Adrian, Charles, and Charles Press. 1977. *Governing Urban America,* 5th ed. New York: McGraw-Hill.

Advisory Commission on Intergovernmental Relations. 1975. *Property Tax Circuit-Breakers: Current Status and Policy Issues.* Washington, D.C.

_____. 1982. *Changing Public Attitudes on Government and Taxes.* Washington, D.C.

Agnew, John. 1980. "Overview," in John Agnew, ed., *Innovation Research and Public Policy.* Syracuse, N.Y.: Syracuse University, pp. 7–12.

Alexander, Herbert. 1972. *Money in Politics.* Washington, D.C.: Public Affairs Press.

_____. 1976. Introduction, "Rethinking Reform," in Herbert Alexander, ed., *Campaign Money: Reform and Reality in the States.* New York: Free Press, pp. 1–13.

_____. 1980. *Financing Politics,* 2nd ed. Washington, D.C.: Congressional Quarterly.

_____. 1984. *Financing Politics.* 3rd ed. Washington, D.C.: Congressional Quarterly.

Allen, Benjamin, and David Vellenga. 1983. "Public Financing of Railroads Under the New Federalism: The Progress and Problems of Selected State Programs." *Transportation Journal* 23: 5–19.

Alston, Liviu. 1984. *Railways and Energy.* Washington, D.C.: World Bank.

Amtrak National Train Timetables. 1985. Washington, D.C.: National Railroad Passenger Corporation, April 28.

Anderson, James. 1984. *Public Policy Making,* 3rd ed. New York: Holt, Rinehart and Winston.

Anton, Thomas. 1966. *The Politics of State Expenditures in Illinois.* Urbana: University of Illinois.

Aronson, J. Richard. 1985. *Public Finance.* New York: McGraw-Hill.

Asher, Herbert. 1980. *Presidential Elections and American Politics,* rev. ed. Homewood, Ill.: Dorsey.

_____. 1984. *Presidential Elections and American Politics,* 3rd ed. Homewood, Ill.: Dorsey.

Axelrod, Robert. 1967. "The Structure of Public Opinion on Policy Issues." *Public Opinion Quarterly* 31: 51–60.

Bachrach, Peter, and Morton Baratz. 1962. "Two Faces of Power. *American Political Science Review* 58: 947–952.

_____. 1970. *Power and Poverty.* New York: Oxford.

Backstrom, Charles, and Gerald Hursh-Cesar. 1981. *Survey Research,* 2nd ed. New York: Wiley.

Bailey, Kenneth. 1982. *Methods of Social Research,* 2nd ed. New York: Free Press.

Bardo, John, and John Hartman. 1982. *Urban Sociology.* Itasca, Ill.: Peacock.

Barnard, Chester. 1938. *The Functions of the Executive.* Cambridge, Mass.: Harvard.

Barnett, H. G. 1953. *Innovation.* New York: McGraw-Hill.

Berland, Lisa. 1983. "Teachers: A Question of Competence." *State Legislatures* 9: 11–15.

Bibby, John, Cornelius Cotter, James Gibson, and Robert Huckshorn. 1983. "Parties in State Politics," in Virginia Gray, Herbert Jacob, and Kenneth Vines, eds., *Politics in the American States,* 4th ed. Boston: Little, Brown, pp. 59–96.

Bingham, Richard. 1976. *The Adoption of Innovation by Local Government.* Lexington, Mass.: Lexington.

Black, William, and James Runke. 1975. *The States and Rural Rail Preservation.* Lexington, Ky.: Council of State Governments.

Blalock, Hubert. 1979. *Social Statistics,* rev. 2nd ed. New York: McGraw-Hill.

Bohrnstedt, George, and David Knoke. 1982. *Statistics for Social Data Analysis.* Itasca, Ill.: Peacock.

Book of the States. 1980, 1982, 1984, 1986. Lexington, Ky.: Council of State Governments.

Booms, Bernard, and James Halldorson. 1973. "The Politics of Redistribution: A Reformulation." *American Political Science Review* 67: 924–933.

Bowersox, Donald, Pat Calabro, and George Wagenheim. 1981. *Introduction to Transportation.* New York: Macmillan.

Bradley, Rodger. 1985. *Amtrak.* Poole, United Kingdom: Blandford.

Break, George. 1980. *Financing Government in a Federal System.* Washington, D.C.: Brookings.

Brewer, Garry, and Peter deLeon. 1983. *The Foundations of Policy Analysis.* Homewood, Ill.: Dorsey.

Buchanan, James, and Marilyn Flowers. 1987. *The Public Finances,* 6th ed. Homewood, Ill.: Irwin.

Burnham, Walter. 1970. *Critical Elections and the Mainsprings of American Politics.* New York: Norton.

Caldeira, Gregory, and Samuel Patterson, 1982. "Contextual Influences on Participation in U.S. State Legislative Elections." *Legislative Studies Quarterly* 7: 359–383.

Cameron, David. 1978. "The Expansion of the Public Economy: A Comparative Analysis." *American Political Science Review* 72: 1243–1261.

Castles, Francis. 1982. "The Impact of Parties on Public Expenditures," in Francis Castles, ed., *The Impact of Parties.* Beverly Hills: Sage, pp. 21–96.

Chance, William. 1986. *The Best of Educations.* Chicago: MacArthur Foundation.

Chelf, Carl. 1981. *Public Policymaking in America.* Santa Monica, Calif.: Goodyear.

Cobb, Roger, and Charles Elder. 1972. *Participation in American Politics.* Baltimore: Johns Hopkins.

Cochran, Clarke, Lawrence Mayer, T. R. Carr, and N. Joseph Cayer. 1982. *American Public Policy.* New York: St. Martin's Press.

Cohen, Michael, James March, and Johan Olsen. 1972. "A Garbage Can Model of Organizational Choice." *Administrative Science Quarterly* 17: 1–25.

Colcord, Frank. 1979. "Urban Transportation and Political Ideology: Sweden and the United States," in Alan Altshuler, ed., *Current Issues in Transportation Policy.* Lexington, Mass.: Lexington, 3–16.

Conant, Michael. 1964. *Railroad Mergers and Abandonments.* Berkeley: University of California.

Congressional Quarterly Almanac. 1972. Washington, D.C.: Congressional Quarterly.

Converse, Philip. 1964. "The Nature of Belief Systems in Mass Publics," in David Apter, ed., *Ideology and Discontent.* New York: Free Press, pp. 206–261.

Cowart, Andrew. 1969. "Anti-Poverty Expenditures in the American States: A Comparative Analysis." *Midwest Journal of Political Science* 13: 219–236.

Coyle, John, Edward Bardi, and Joseph Cavinato. 1982. *Transportation.* St. Paul: West.

Crane, Edgar. 1977. *Legislative Review of Government Programs.* New York: Praeger.

Craven, E. R. 1977. "Electrification and Railroad Organization and Operations," in *Railroad Electrification: The Issues.* Special Report 180. Washington, D.C.: National Academy of Sciences, pp. 13–15.

Crecine, John. 1969. *Governmental Problem Solving.* Chicago: Rand McNally.

Creger, Ralph, and Barry Combs. 1981. *Train Power.* Independence, Mo.: Independence Press.

Crenson, Matthew. 1971. The Un-Politics of Air Pollution. Baltimore: Johns Hopkins.

Crotty, William, and Gary Jacobson. 1980. *American Parties in Decline.* Boston: Little, Brown.

Cyert, Richard, and James March. 1963. *A Behavioral Theory of the Firm.* Englewood Cliffs, N.J.: Prentice-Hall.

DeClercq, Eugene, Thomas Hurley, and Norman Luttbeg. 1981. "Voting in American Presidential Elections, 1956–1976," in Norman Luttbeg, ed., *Public Opinion and Public Policy,* 3rd ed. Itasca, Ill.: Peacock, pp. 28–43.

DeLeon, Richard. 1973. "Politics, Economic Surplus, and Redistribution in the American States: A Test of a Theory." *American Journal of Political Science* 17: 781–796.

Derthick, Martha. 1975. *Uncontrollable Spending for Social Services Grants.* Washington, D.C.: Brookings.

Dolbeare, Kenneth, and Patricia Dolbeare. 1976. *American Ideologies,* 3rd ed. Boston: Houghton Mifflin.

Downs, Anthony. 1957. *An Economic Theory of Democracy.* New York: Harper and Row.

——. 1967. *Inside Bureaucracy.* Boston: Little, Brown.

Downs, George. 1976. *Bureaucracy, Innovation, and Public Policy.* Lexington, Mass.: Lexington.

Downs, George, and Lawrence Mohr. 1980. "Toward a Theory of Innovation," in John Agnew, ed., *Innovation Research and Public Policy.* Syracuse, N.Y.: Syracuse University, pp. 75–100.

Drury, George. 1985. *The Historical Guide to North American Railroads.* Milwaukee: Kalmbach.

Dunn, Delmer. 1972. *Financing Presidential Campaigns.* Washington, D.C.: Brookings.

Dye, Thomas. 1966. *Politics, Economics, and the Public.* Chicago: Rand McNally.

——. 1969. "Income Inequality and American State Politics." *American Political Science Review* 63: 157–162.

——. 1980. "Taxing, Spending, and Economic Growth in the American States." *Journal of Politics* 42: 1085–1107.

——. 1981. *Politics in States and Communities,* 4th ed. Englewood Cliffs, N.J.: Prentice-Hall.

——. 1984. *Understanding Public Policy,* 5th ed. Englewood Cliffs, N.J.: Prentice-Hall.

——. 1987. *Understanding Public Policy,* 6th ed. Englewood Cliffs, N.J.: Prentice-Hall.

——. 1988. *Politics in States and Communities,* 6th ed. Englewood Cliffs, N.J.: Prentice-Hall.

Economic ABZ's of the Railroad Industry. 1980. Washington, D.C.: Association of American Railroads.

Edelman, Murray. 1964. *The Symbolic Uses of Politics.* Urbana: University of Illinois.

Edwards, George, and Ira Sharkansky. 1978. *The Policy Predicament.* San Francisco: Freeman.

Elazar, Daniel. 1972. *American Federalism,* 2nd ed. New York: Crowell.

Eldersveld, Samuel. 1982. *Political Parties in American Society.* New York: Basic.

Erickson, Robert. 1976. "The Relationship Between Public Opinion and State Policy: A New Look Based on Some Forgotten Data." *American Journal of Political Science* 20: 25–36.

Erickson, Robert, Norman Luttbeg, and Kent Tedin. 1980. *American Public Opinion,* 2nd ed. New York: Wiley.

Ethridge, Marcus. 1981. "Legislative-Administrative Interaction as 'Intrusive Access': An Empirical Analysis." *Journal of Politics* 43: 473–492.

Eyestone, Robert. 1977. "Confusion, Diffusion, and Innovation." *American Political Science Review,* 71: 441–447.

Falwell, Jerry. 1984. "Certain Forms of Sexuality Should be Illegal to Protect Individuals and Society," in Harold Feldman and Andrea Parrot, eds., *Human Sexuality.* Beverly Hills, Calif.: Sage, pp. 294–301.

Feeley, Malcolm, and Samuel Krislov, 1990. *Constitutional Law,* 2nd ed. Glenview, Ill.: Scott, Foresman; Little, Brown.

Fesler, James. 1980. *Public Administration.* Englewood Cliffs, N.J.: Prentice-Hall.

Fiorina, Morris. 1981. "Congressional Control of the Bureaucracy: A Mismatch of Incentives and Capabilities," in Lawrence Dodd and Bruce Oppenheimer, eds., *Congress Reconsidered,* 2nd ed. Washington, D.C.: Congressional Quarterly, pp. 332–348.

Fleischmann, Arnold, and David Nice. 1988. "States and PACs: The Legacy of Established Decision Rules," *Political Behavior* 10: 349–363.

Fling, Karen. 1979. "The States as Laboratories of Reform," in Herbert Alexander, ed., *Political Finance.* Beverly Hills, Calif.: Sage, pp. 245–270.

Flinn, Thomas, and Frederick Wirt. 1965. "Local Party Leaders: Groups of Like-minded Men." *Midwest Journal of Political Science* 9: 77–98.

Friedman, Robert. 1971. "State Politics and Highways," in Herbert Jacob and Kenneth Vines, eds., *Politics in the American States,* 2nd. ed. Boston: Little, Brown, pp. 477–519.

Friesema, H. Paul, and Ronald Hedlund. 1981. "The Reality of Representational Roles," in Norman Luttbeg, ed., *Public Opinion and Public Policy,* 3rd ed. Itasca, Ill.: Peacock, pp. 316–320.

Gallup Report. 1985a. No. 238: July.

Gallup Report. 1985b. No. 240: September.

Gallup Report. 1986a. January–February.

Gallup Report. 1986b. June.

Gamson, William. 1975. *The Strategy of Social Protest.* Homewood, Ill.: Dorsey.

Gardiner, Paul. 1978. "National Transportation Policy and National Defense: Partners or Apart?" in *Proceedings of the Transportation Research Forum,* 19. Oxford, Ind.: Richard B. Cross, pp. 12–19.

Glantz, Stanton, Alan Abramowitz, and Michael Burkart. 1976. "Election Outcomes: Whose Money Matters?" *Journal of Politics* 38: 1033–1038.

Glendening, Parris, and Mavis Reeves. 1984. *Pragmatic Federalism,* 2nd ed. Pacific Palisades, Calif.: Palisades.

Gold, Steven. 1979. *Property Tax Relief.* Lexington, Mass.: Lexington.

Goldman, Sheldon, and Thomas Jahnige. 1985. *The Federal Courts as a Political System,* 3rd ed. New York: Harper and Row.

Gramlich, Edward. 1981. *Benefit-Cost Analysis of Government Programs.* Englewood Cliffs, N.J.: Prentice-Hall.

Grant, Daniel, and H. C. Nixon. 1975. *State and Local Government in America,* 3rd ed. Boston: Allyn and Bacon.

———. 1982. *State and Local Government in America,* 4th ed. Boston: Allyn and Bacon.

Grant, Daniel, and Lloyd Omdahl. 1987. *State and Local Government in America,* 5th ed. Boston: Allyn and Bacon.

Grant, W. Vance, and Leo Eiden. 1982. *Digest of Education Statistics.* Washington, D.C.: National Center for Education Statistics.

Gray, Virginia. 1973. "Innovation in the States: A Diffusion Study." *American Political Science Review* 67: 1174–1185.

Green, Donald, and Jonathan Krasno. 1988. "Salvation for the Spendthrift Incumbent: Reestimating the Effects of Campaign Spending in House Elections." *American Journal of Political Science* 32: 884–907.

Greenwald, Carol. 1977. *Group Power.* New York: Praeger.

Grodzins, Morton. 1984. *The American System,* ed. Daniel Elazar. New Brunswick, N.J.: Transaction.

Hall, Richard. 1977. *Organizations,* 2nd ed. Englewood Cliffs, N.J.: Prentice-Hall.

Hamm, Keith, and Roby Robertson. 1981. "Factors Influencing the Adoption of New Methods of Legislative Oversight in the U.S. States." *Legislative Studies Quarterly* 6: 133–150.

Hanson, Russell. 1983. "The Intergovernmental Setting of State Politics," in Virginia Gray, Herbert Jacob, and Kenneth Vines, eds., *Politics in the American States,* 4th ed. Boston: Little, Brown, pp. 27–56.

Hapgood, David. 1976. "The Highwaymen," in Charles Peters and James Fallows, eds., *Inside the System,* 3rd ed. New York: Praeger, pp. 249–259.

Harper, Donald. 1982. *Transportation in America,* 2nd ed. Englewood Cliffs, N.J.: Prentice-Hall.

Harris, Joseph. 1964. *Congressional Control of Administration.* Washington, D.C.: Brookings.

Heffernan, Virginia. 1984. "The Primary Purpose of Intercourse is Procreation," in Harold Feldman and Andrea Parrot, eds., *Human Sexuality.* Beverly Hills, Calif.: Sage, pp. 79–88.

Henry, Nicholas. 1984. *Governing at the Grass Roots,* 2nd ed. Englewood Cliffs, N.J.: Prentice-Hall.

Hibbs, Douglas. 1977. "Political Parties and Macroeconomic Policy," *American Political Science Review* 71: 1467–1487.

Hill, David, and Norman Luttbeg. 1983. *Trends in American Electoral Behavior.* Itasca, Ill.: Peacock.

Hilton, George. 1980. *Amtrak.* Washington, D.C.: American Enterprise Institute.

Hofferbert, Richard, and John Urice. 1985. "Small-Scale Policy: The Federal Stimulus versus Competing Explanations for State Funding of the Arts." *American Journal of Political Science* 29: 308–329.

Hollingsworth, J. B., and P. B. Whitehouse. 1977. *American Railroads.* London: Bison.

Hopkins, Anne. 1974. "Opinions Publics and Support for Public Policy in the American States." *American Journal of Political Science* 18: 167–178.

Jacobson, Gary. 1980. *Money in Congressional Elections.* New Haven: Yale.

Jacobson, Gary, and Samuel Kernell. 1981. *Strategy and Choice in Congressional Elections.* New Haven, Conn.: Yale.

Jennings, Edward. 1979. "Competition, Constituencies, and Welfare Policies in American States." *American Political Science Review* 73: 414–429.

Jennings, M. Kent, and L. Harmon Ziegler, 1970. "The Salience of American State Politics." *American Political Science Review* 64: 523–535.

Jewell, Malcolm. 1969. *The State Legislature,* 2nd ed. New York: Random House.

Jones, Charles. 1976. "Regulating the Environment," in Herbert Jacob and Kenneth Vines, eds. *Politics in the American States,* 3rd ed. Boston: Little, Brown, pp. 388–427.

_____. 1984. *An Introduction to the Study of Public Policy,* 3rd ed. Monterey, Calif.: Brooks/Cole.

Jones, Ruth. 1980. "State Public Financing and the State Parties," in Michael Malbin, ed., *Parties, Interest Groups and Campaign Finance Laws.* Washington, D.C.: American Enterprise Institute, pp. 282–303.

_____. 1981. "State Public Campaign Finance: Implications for Partisan Politics." *American Journal of Political Science,* 25: 342–361.

Katz, Daniel, Barbara Gutek, Robert Kahn, and Eugenia Barton. 1975. *Bureaucratic Encounters.* Ann Arbor: Institute for Social Research, University of Michigan.

Kaufman, Herbert. 1976. *Are Government Organizations Immortal?* Washington, D.C.: Brookings.

Keefe, William. 1966. "The Functions and Powers of the State Legislatures," in Alexander Heard, ed. *State Legislatures in American Politics.* Englewood Cliffs, N.J.: Prentice-Hall, pp. 37–69.

Keefe, William, and Morris Ogul. 1985. *The American Legislative Process,* 6th ed. Englewood Cliffs, N.J.: Prentice-Hall.

Keeler, Theodore. 1983. *Railroads, Freight, and Public Policy.* Washington, D.C.: Brookings.

Kerlinger, Fred, and Elazar Pedhazur. 1973. *Multiple Regression in Behavioral Research.* New York: Holt, Rinehart and Winston.

Key, V. O. 1949. *Southern Politics.* New York: Vintage.

Kim, Jae-on, John Petrocik, and Stephen Enokson. 1975. "Voter Turnout Among the American States: Systemic and Individual Components." *American Political Science Review* 69: 107–123.

Kingdon, John. 1981. *Congressmen's Voting Decisions,* 2nd ed. New York: Harper and Row.

———. 1984. *Agendas, Alternatives, and Public Policies.* Boston: Little, Brown.

Kinsey, Alfred, Wardell Pomercy, and Clyde Martin. 1948. *Sexual Behavior in the Human Male.* Philadelphia: Saunders.

Klingman, David, and William Lammers. 1984. "The General Policy Liberalism Factor in American State Politics." *American Journal of Political Science* 28: 598–610.

Klecka, William. 1980. *Discriminant Analysis.* Beverly Hills, Calif.: Sage.

Kogan, Benjamin. 1973. *Human Sexual Expression.* New York: Harcourt Brace Jovanovich.

Kopel, Gerald. 1976. "Sunset in the West." *State Government* 49: 135–138.

Ladd, Everett. 1982. *Where Have All the Voters Gone?* 2nd ed. New York: Norton.

Levine, Charles. 1980. *Managing Fiscal Stress.* Chatham, N.J.: Chatham.

Lewis, Edward. 1986. *American Shortline Railway Guide,* 3rd ed. Milwaukee: Kalmbach.

Limitations on State Deficits. 1976. Lexington, Ky.: Council of State Governments.

Lindblom, Charles. 1959. "The Science of Muddling Through." *Public Administration Review* 19: 79–88.

Lineberry, Robert. 1978. *American Public Policy.* New York: Harper and Row.

Lipsky, Michael. 1980. *Street Level Bureaucracy.* New York: Russel Sage.

Lockard, Duane. 1963. *The Politics of State and Local Government.* New York: Macmillan.

Locklin, D. Philip. 1972. *Economics of Transportation,* 7th ed. Homewood, Ill.: Irwin.

Lowery, David. 1982. "Public Choice When Services Are Costs: The Divergent Case of Assessment Administration." *American Journal of Political Science* 26: 57–76.

———. 1984. "Tax Equity Under Conditions of Fiscal Stress: The Case of the Property Tax." *Publius* 14: 55–66.

———. 1985. "The Keynesian and Political Determinants of Unbalanced Budgets: U.S. Fiscal Policy from Eisenhower to Reagan." *American Journal of Political Science* 29: 428–460.

Lowi, Theodore. 1968. "Foreword to the Second Edition: Gosnell's Chicago Revisited Via Lindsay's New York," in Harold Gosnell, *Machine Politics: Chicago Model,* 2nd ed. Chicago: University of Chicago, pp. v–xviii.

Maddox, Russell, and Robert Fuquay. 1981. *State and Local Government,* 4th ed. New York: Van Nostrand.

Malbin, Michael. 1980. "Of Mountains and Molehills: PACs, Campaigns, and Public Policy," in Michael Malbin, ed., *Parties, Interest Groups and Campaign Finance Laws.* Washington, D.C.: American Enterprise Institute, pp. 152–184.

March, James, and Herbert Simon. 1958. *Organizations.* New York: Wiley.

Martin, Roscoe. 1965. *The Cities and the Federal System.* New York: Atherton.

Maxwell, James, and J. Richard Aronson. 1977. *Financing State and Local Governments,* 3rd ed. Washington, D.C.: Brookings.

Mayhew, David. 1966. *Party Loyalty Among Congressmen.* Cambridge, Mass.: Harvard.

———. 1974. *Congress: The Electoral Connection.* New Haven, Conn.: Yale.

Maze, T. H., Allen Cook, and Max Carter. 1984. "Restoring Rail Service Along the Old Chisolm Trail: The Oklahoma Brokerage Approach." *Transportation Journal* 23: 15–23.

McCary, James. 1973. *Human Sexuality,* 2nd ed. New York: Van Nostrand.

McGregor, Eugene. 1978. "Uncertainty and National Nominating Coalitions." *Journal of Politics* 40: 1011–1043.

Meier, Kenneth. 1985. *Regulation.* New York: St. Martin's Press.

Merriam, Charles. 1922. *The American Party System.* New York: Macmillan.

Merton, Robert. 1965. "The Environment of the Innovating Organizations: Some Conjectures and Proposals," in Gary Steiner, ed., *The Creative Organization.* Chicago: University of Chicago, pp. 50–62.

Mikesell, John. 1982. *Fiscal Administration.* Homewood, Ill.: Dorsey.

Mohr, Lawrence. 1969. "Determinants of Innovation in Organization." *American Political Science Review* 63: 111–126.

———. 1988. *Impact Analysis for Program Evaluation.* Chicago: Dorsey.

Moore, James. 1969. "Problematic Sexual Behavior," in Carlfred Broderick and Jessie Bernard, eds., *The Individual, Sex, and Society.* Baltimore: Johns Hopkins, pp. 343–372.

Morris, Inez, and David Morris. 1977. *North America by Rail.* Indianapolis: Bobbs-Merrill.

Moynihan, Daniel. 1970. *Maximum Feasible Misunderstanding.* New York: Free Press.

Mulvey, Francis. 1979. "Amtrak: A Cost Effectiveness Analysis." *Transportation Research, Part A: General* 13: 329–344.

Munger, Frank, and James Blackhurst. 1965. "Factionalism in the National Conventions, 1940–1964: An Analysis of Ideological Consistency in State Delegation Voting." *Journal of Politics* 27: 375–394.

Musgrave, Richard, and Peggy Musgrave. 1980. *Public Finance in Theory and Practice,* 3rd ed. New York: McGraw-Hill.

A Nation at Risk. 1983. Washington, D.C.: National Commission on Excellence in Education.

The Nation Responds. 1984. Washington, D.C.: U.S. Department of Education.

National Taxpayers Union. 1984. Personal communication.

National Transportation Statistics. 1980. Washington, D.C.: U.S. Department of Transportation.

Netzer, Dick. 1966. *The Economics of the Property Tax.* Washington, D.C.: Brookings.

Nice, David. 1979. "The Impact of Barriers to Party Government in the American States." Ph.D. diss., University of Michigan.

————. 1982. "Party Ideology and Policy Outcomes in the American States." *Social Science Quarterly* 63: 556–565.

————. 1983a. "Representation in the States: Policymaking and Ideology." *Social Quarterly* 64: 404–411.

————. 1983b. "Political Corruption in the American States." *American Politics Quarterly* 11: 507–517.

————. 1983c. "Amtrak in the States." *Policy Studies Journal* 11: 587–597.

————. 1985a. "State Party Ideology and Policy Making." *Policy Studies Journal* 13: 780–796.

————. 1985b. "Sunset Laws and Legislative Vetos in the States." *State Government* 58: 27–32.

————. 1986. "State Opposition to the Equal Rights Amendment: Protectionism, Subordination, or Privatization?" *Social Science Quarterly,* 67: 315–328.

————. 1987a. "State and Local Government Ownership of Freight Railroads." *Transportation Quarterly* 41: 587–600.

————. 1987b. Incremental and Nonincremental Policy Responses: The States and the Railroads." *Polity* 20: 145–156.

————. 1987c. *Federalism.* New York: St. Martin's Press.

————. 1987d. "Campaign Spending and Presidential Election Results." *Polity* 19: 464–476.

————. 1988a. "Program Survival and Termination: State Subsidies of Amtrak." *Transportation Quarterly* 42: 571–585.

————. 1988b. "Abortion Clinic Bombings as Political Violence." *American Journal of Political Science* 32: 178–195.

Nice, David, and Jeffrey Cohen. 1983. "Ideology Consistency Among State Party Delegations to the U.S. House, Senate, and National Conventions." *Social Science Quarterly* 64: 871–879.

Nie, Norman, Sidney Verba, and John Petrocik. 1976. *The Changing American Voter.* Cambridge, Mass.: Harvard.

Nigro, Felix, and Lloyd Nigro. 1980. *Modern Public Administration,* 5th ed. New York: Harper and Row.

Ogul, Morris. 1976. *Congress Oversees the Bureaucracy.* Pittsburgh: University of Pittsburgh.

Olson, Mancur. 1965. *The Logic of Collective Action.* Cambridge, Mass.: Harvard.

Ornstein, Norman, and Shirley Elder. 1978. *Interest Groups, Lobbying, and Policymaking.* Washington, D.C.: Congressional Quarterly.

Ostrom, Charles, and Dennis Simon. 1985. "Promise and Performance: A Dynamic Model of Presidential Popularity." *American Political Science Review* 79: 334–358.

Paul, Daine. 1975. *The Politics of the Property Tax.* Lexington, Mass.: Lexington.

Pegrum, Dudley. 1973. *Transportation: Economics and Public Policy.* Homewood, Ill.: Irwin.

Penne, R. Leo, and Paul Verduin. 1986. *State Government Association: A Reconnaissance.* Washington, D.C.: National League of Cities.

Peters, B. Guy. 1986. *American Public Policy,* 2nd ed. Chatham, N.J.: Chatham House.

Peters, John, and Susan Welch. 1978. "Politics, Corruption, and Political Culture." *American Politics Quarterly* 6: 345–356.

Peterson, George. 1976. "Finance," in William Gorham and Nathan Glazer, eds., *The Urban Predicament.* Washington, D.C.: Urban Institute, pp. 35–118.

Peterson, George, Arthur Solomon, Hadi Madjid, and William Apgar. 1973. *Property Taxes, Housing, and the Cities.* Lexington, Mass.: Lexington.

Pierce, John, Kathleen Beatty, and Paul Hagner. 1982. *The Dynamics of American Public Opinion.* Glenview, Ill.: Scott, Foresman.

Plotnick, Robert, and Richard Winters. 1985. "A Politicoeconomic Theory of Income Redistribution." *American Political Science Review* 79: 458–473.

Polsby, Nelson. 1984. *Political Innovation in America.* New Haven, Conn.: Yale.

Pound, William. 1982. "The State Legislatures," in *The Book of the States.* Lexington, Ky.: Council of State Governments, pp. 181–187.

Press, Aric, Ann McDaniel, George Raine, and Ginny Carroll. 1986. "A Government in the Bedroom." *Newsweek* (July 14): 36–38.

Press, Charles, and Kenneth VerBurg. 1983. *State and Community Governments in the Federal System,* 2nd ed. New York: Wiley.

Presthus, Robert. 1978. *The Organizational Society,* rev. ed. New York: St. Martin's Press.

Pritchett, C. Herman. 1977. *The American Constitution,* 3rd ed. New York: McGraw-Hill.

Railroad Facts. 1984. Washington, D.C.: Association of American Railroads.

Railway Age. 1986. "Coal Fueled Power: An Assist from DOE." December, p. 24.

Ranney, Austin. 1976. "Parties in State Politics," in Herbert Jacob and Kenneth Vines, eds., *Politics in the American States,* 3rd ed. Boston: Little, Brown, pp. 51–92.

Report on an Evaluation of the 50 State Legislatures. 1971. Kansas City, Mo.: Citizens' Conference on State Legislatures.

Rogers, Everett. 1983. *Diffusion of Innovations,* 3rd ed. New York: Free Press.

Rose, Richard. 1974. *The Problem of Party Government.* London: Macmillan.

Rosen, Harvey. 1985. *Public Finance.* Homewood, Ill.: Irwin.

Rosenblatt, Jean. 1985. "Post-Sputnik Education," in *Education Report Card.* Washington, D.C.: Congressional Quarterly, pp. 65–84.

Rosenthal, Alan. 1981. *Legislative Life.* New York: Harper and Row.

Rossi, Peter, and Howard Freeman. 1982. *Evaluation.* Beverly Hills, Calif.: Sage.

Rourke, Francis. 1984. *Bureaucracy, Politics, and Public Policy,* 3rd ed. Boston: Little, Brown.

Sabato, Larry. 1984. *PAC Power.* New York: Norton.

Sampson, Roy, and Martin Farris. 1979. *Domestic Transportation,* 4th ed. Boston: Houghton Mifflin.

Sampson, Roy, Martin Farris, and David Schrock. 1985. *Domestic Transportation,* 5th ed. Boston: Houghton Mifflin.

Sanford, Terry. 1967. *Storm Over the States.* New York: McGraw-Hill.

Sargent, Lyman. 1981. *Contemporary Political Ideologies,* 5th ed. Homewood, Ill.: Dorsey.

Savage, Robert. 1978. "Policy Innovativeness as a Trait of American States." *Journal of Politics* 40: 212–228.

———. 1985. "Diffusion Research Traditions and the Spread of Policy Innovations in a Federal System." *Publius* 15: 1–28.

Scammon, Richard, and Ben Wattenberg. 1970. *The Real Majority.* New York: Coward, McCann and Geohean.

Schattschneider, E. E. 1942. *Party Government.* New York: Holt, Rinehart and Winston.

———. 1960. *The Semisovereign People.* New York: Holt, Rinehart and Winston.

Scher, Seymour. 1963. "Conditions for Legislative Control." *Journal of Politics* 25: 526–551.

Schiermeyer, Carl, and L. Erik Lange. 1988. "The Making of a Corridor." *Passenger Train Journal* 122: 16–21.

Schlozman, Kay. 1984. "What Accent the Heavenly Chorus? Political Equality and the American Pressure System." *Journal of Politics* 46: 1006–1032.

Schwarz, John, and Barton Fenmore. 1977. "Presidential Election Results and Congressional Roll Call Behavior: The Cases of 1964, 1968, and 1972." *Legislative Studies Quarterly* 2: 409–422.

Seidman, Harold. 1975. *Politics, Position, and Power,* 2nd ed. New York: Oxford.

Shannon, John, and Bruce Wallin. 1979. "Restraining the Federal Budget: Alternative politics and Strategies." *Intergovernmental Perspective* 5: 8–14.

Sharkansky, Ira. 1968. *Spending in the American States.* Chicago: Rand McNally.

———. 1969. "The Utility of Elazar's Political Culture." *Polity* 2: 66–83.

———. 1970. *The Routines of Politics.* New York: Van Nostrand.

———. 1978. *The Maligned States,* 2nd ed. New York: McGraw-Hill.

Sharkansky, Ira, and Richard Hofferbert. 1971. "Dimensions of State Policy," in Herbert Jacob and Kenneth Vines, eds., *Politics in the American States,* 2nd ed. Boston: Little, Brown, pp. 315–353.

Sharp, Ansel, and Kent Olson. 1978. *Public Finance.* St. Paul: West.

Shimberg, Benjamin. 1976. "The Sunset Approach: Key to Regulatory Reform." *State Government* 49: 140–147.

Shulman, Max. 1954. *Rally Round the Flag Boys.* Garden City, N.Y.: Doubleday.

Sibley, Mulford. 1970. *Political Ideas and Ideologies.* New York: Harper and Row.

Simon, Herbert, Donald Smithburg, and Victor Thompson. 1950. *Public Administration*. New York: Knopf.

Sorauf, Frank. 1980. *Party Politics in America,* 4th ed. Boston: Little, Brown.

_____. 1984. *Party Politics in America,* 5th ed. Boston: Little, Brown.

Starbuck, William. 1965. "Organizational Growth and Development," in James March, ed., *Handbook of Organizations.* Chicago: Rand McNally, pp. 451–533.

Statistical Abstract. 1974, 1980, 1982. Washington, D.C.: Bureau of the Census.

Stein, Robert. 1984. "State Regulation and the Political Consequences of Urban Fiscal Stress." *Publis* 14: 41–54.

Stein, Robert, Keith Hamm, and Patricia Freeman, 1983. "An Analysis of Support for Tax Limitation Referenda." *Public Choice* 40: 187–194.

Stover, John. 1961. *American Railroads.* Chicago: University of Chicago.

Sullivan, John. 1973. "Political Correlates of Social, Economic, and Religious Diversity in the American States." *Journal of Politics* 35: 70–84.

Sundquist, James. 1968. *Politics and Policy.* Washington, D.C.: Brookings.

Sundquist, James, and David Davis. 1969. *Making Federalism Work.* Washington, D.C.: Brookings.

Sutton, Richard. 1973. "The States and the People: Measuring and Accounting for State Representativeness." *Polity* 5: 452–476.

Thompson, Dennis. 1981. *Taxation of American Railroads.* Westport, Conn.: Greenwood.

Thompson, Roger. 1985a. "Teachers: The Push for Excellence," in *Education Report Card.* Washington, D.C.: Congressional Quarterly, pp. 45–64.

_____. 1985b. "The Status of the Schools," in *Education Report Card,* pp. 1–24.

Thompson, Victor. 1969. *Bureaucracy and Innovation.* University: University of Alabama.

Thoreau, Henry. 1976. *Walden.* Secaucus, N.J.: Longriver.

Tufte, Edward. 1978. *Political Control of the Economy.* Princeton, N.J.: Princeton.

Verba, Sidney, and Norman Nie. 1972. *Participation in America.* New York: Harper and Row.

Walker, Jack. 1969. "The Diffusion of Innovations Among the American States." *American Political Science Review* 63: 880–899.

_____. 1971. "Innovation in State Politics," in Herbert Jacob and Kenneth Vines, eds., *Politics in the American States,* 2nd ed. Boston: Little, Brown, pp. 364–387.

_____. 1977. "Setting the Agenda in the U.S. Senate: A Theory of Problem Selection." *British Journal of Political Science* 7: 423–445.

Warren, William. 1982. "Changes in American Intercity Rail Transportation, 1950–1980." *Transportation Quarterly* 36: 145–160.

Wayne, Stephen. 1980. *The Road to the White House.* New York: St. Martin's Press.

Weber, Ronald, and William Shaffer. 1972. "Public Opinion and American State Policy-Making." *Midwest Journal of Political Science,* 16: 683–699.

Welch, Susan, and Kay Thompson. 1980. "The Impact of Federal Incentives on State Policy Innovation." *American Journal of Political Science* 24: 715–729.

Welch, W. P. 1976. "The Effectiveness of Expenditures in State Legislative Races." *American Politics Quarterly* 4: 333–356.

Wildavsky, Aaron. 1974. *The Politics of the Budgetary Process,* 2nd ed. Boston: Little, Brown.

_____. 1986. *Budgeting,* rev. ed. New Brunswick, N.J.: Transaction.

_____. 1988. *The New Politics of the Budgetary Process.* Glenview, Ill.: Scott, Foresman.

Wirt, Frederick. 1983. "Institutionalization: Prison and School Policies," in Virginia Gray, Herbert Jacob, and Kenneth Vines, eds., *Politics in the American States,* 4th ed. Boston: Little, Brown, pp. 287–328.

Wirt, Frederick, and Samuel Gove. 1990. "Education," in Virginia Gray, Herbert Jacob, and Robert Albritton, eds., *Politics in the American States,* 5th ed. Glenview, Ill.: Scott, Foresman; Little, Brown, pp. 447–478.

Wonnacott, Ronald, and Thomas Wonnacott. 1979. *Econometrics.* New York: Wiley.

Worden, Robert, and Alissa Pollitz Worden. 1986. "Local Politics and Indigent Defense: The Case of Georgia." Paper presented at the 1986 meeting of the American Political Science Association, Washington, D.C.

World Almanac. 1983. New York: Newspaper Enterprise Association.

Wright, Deil. 1967. "Executive Leadership in State Administration." *Midwest Journal of Political Science* 11: 1–26.

_____. 1982. *Understanding Intergovernmental Relations,* 2nd ed. Monterey, Calif.: Brooks/Cole.

Wright, Gerald, Robert Erikson, and John McIver. 1985. "Measuring State Partisanship and Ideology with Survey Data." *Journal of Politics* 47: 469–489.

_____. 1987. "Public Opinion and Policy Liberalism in the American States." *American Journal of Political Science* 31: 980–1001.

Yearbook of Railroad Facts. 1981. Washington, D.C.: Association of American Railroads.

Zaltman, Gerald, Robert Duncan, and Jonny Holbek. 1973. *Innovations and Organizations.* New York: Wiley.

Zeigler, L. Harmon, and Harvey Tucker. 1978. *The Quest for Responsive Government.* North Scituate, Mass.: Duxbury.

INDEX

Page numbers in *italics* refer to tables.